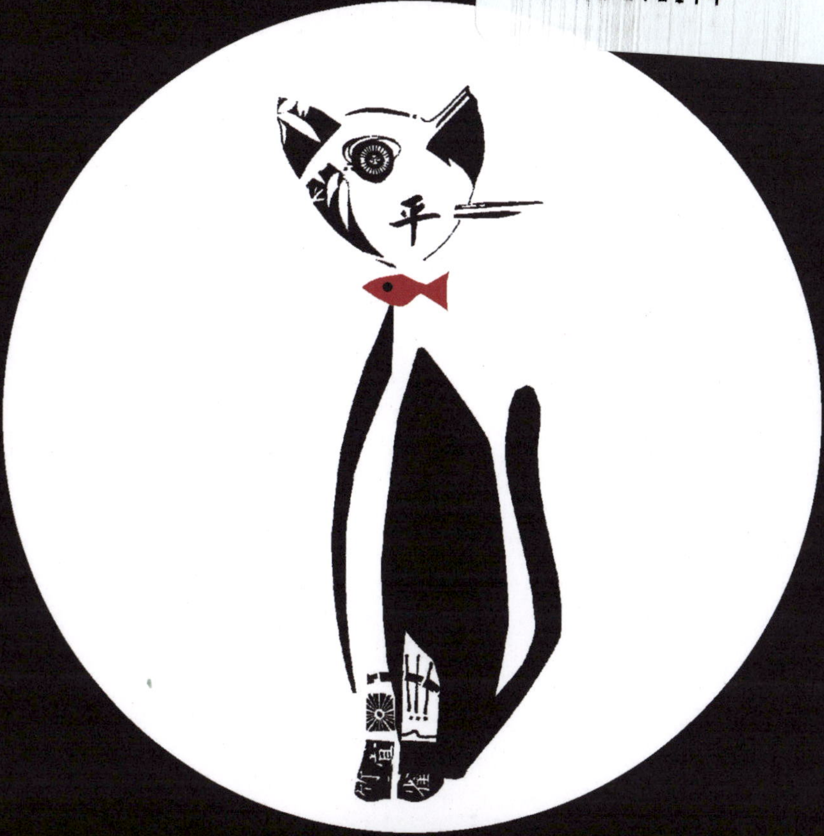

AF378174

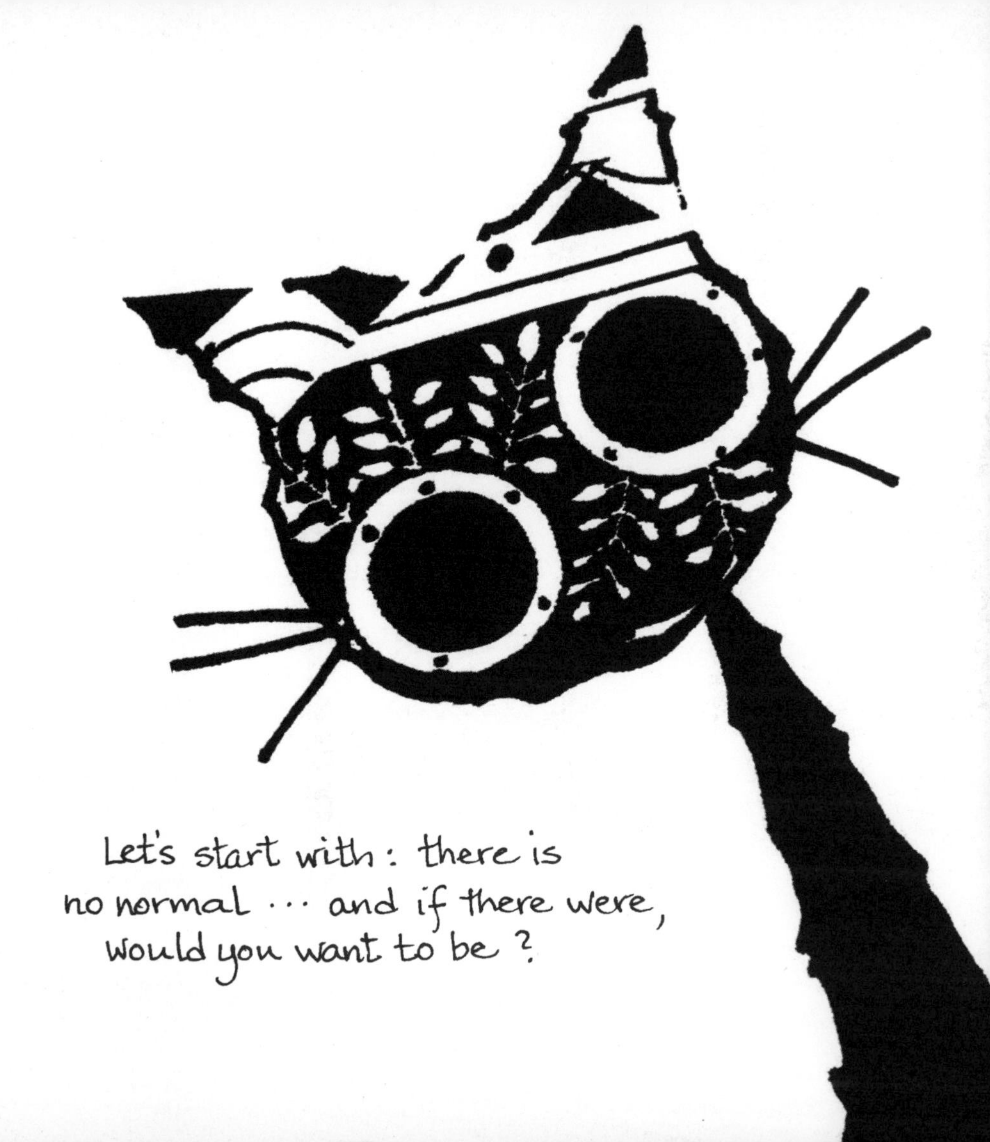

Let's start with: there is
no normal … and if there were,
would you want to be?

HAIKU CATS

Collages and Haiku

by

CBFraser

TUTTLE Publishing

Tokyo | Rutland, Vermont | Singapore

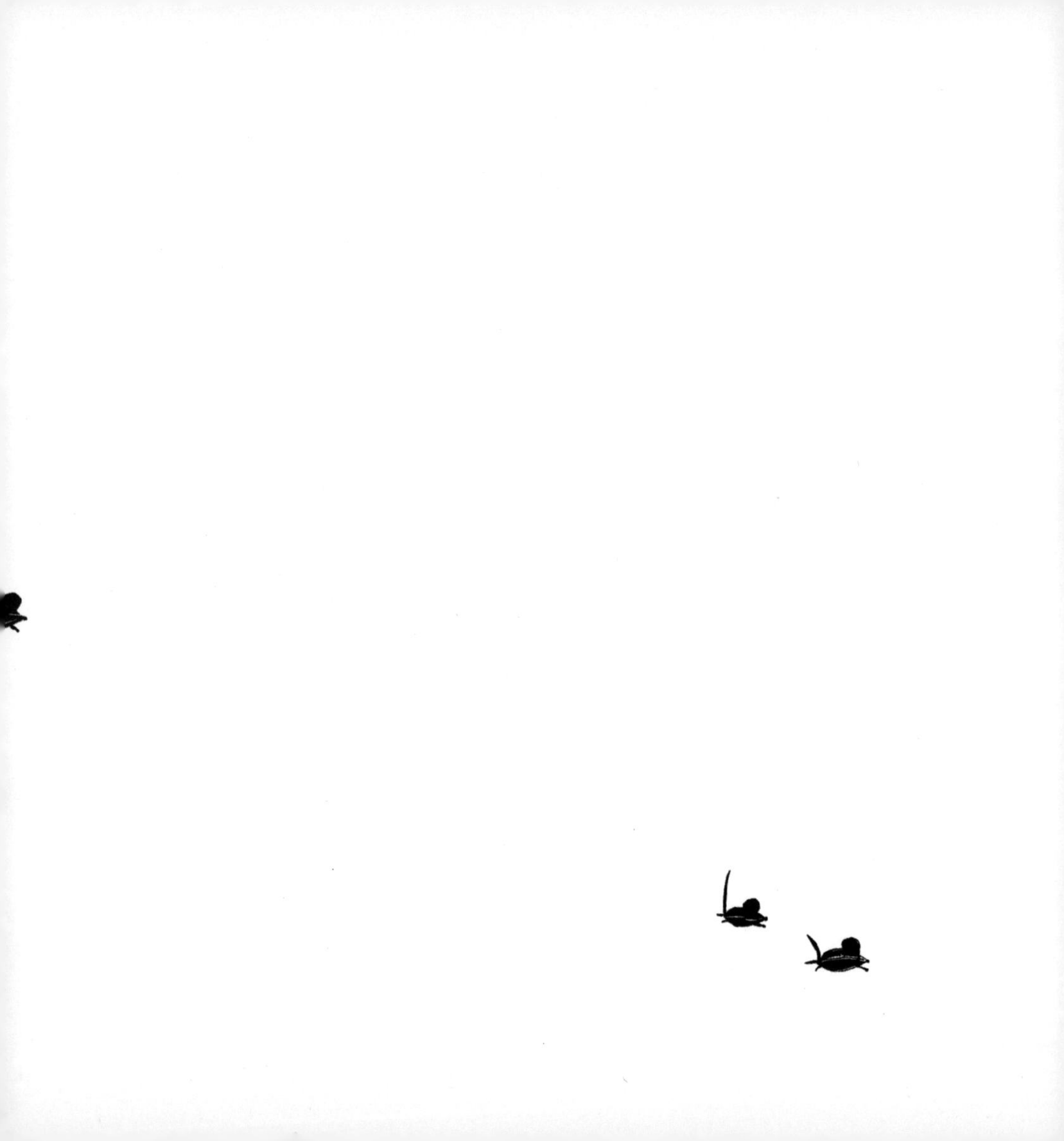

Haiku (hī'koo) n. : Japanese lyric poem of a fixed 17 syllable form that often refers to a thing in nature that has moved the poet

Cats (kăts) pl. n.: nature's emissaries put on earth to enchant, confound, and humble the human race

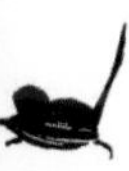

Some years ago, a therapist noted that I had a "very high tolerance for inappropriate behavior in others;" which is no doubt why she suggested I get a cat. My neighbors tabby apparently concurred, and delivered a litter of five on my bed in the wee hours of the morning. Up to that point, I had percieved cats to be only minimally user friendly. Six weeks with five kittens changed this view forever.

Many years and cats down the road, I've now given birth to my own generations of kitties. The collages and haiku in this book are a fusion of my love of felines and my lifelong affinity for Asian design. They are also evidence that I am now that person I promised my sister I would never become: a fringe character keeping company with way too many cats.

CB

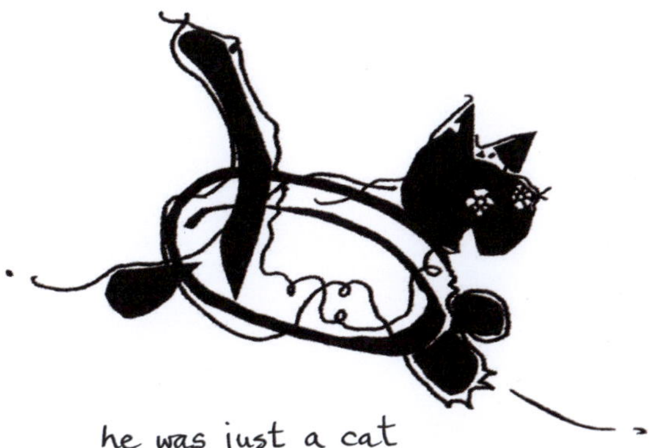

he was just a cat

sweet quirky special — my cat

and I will miss him

something wonderful

is headed your direction

leave the door open

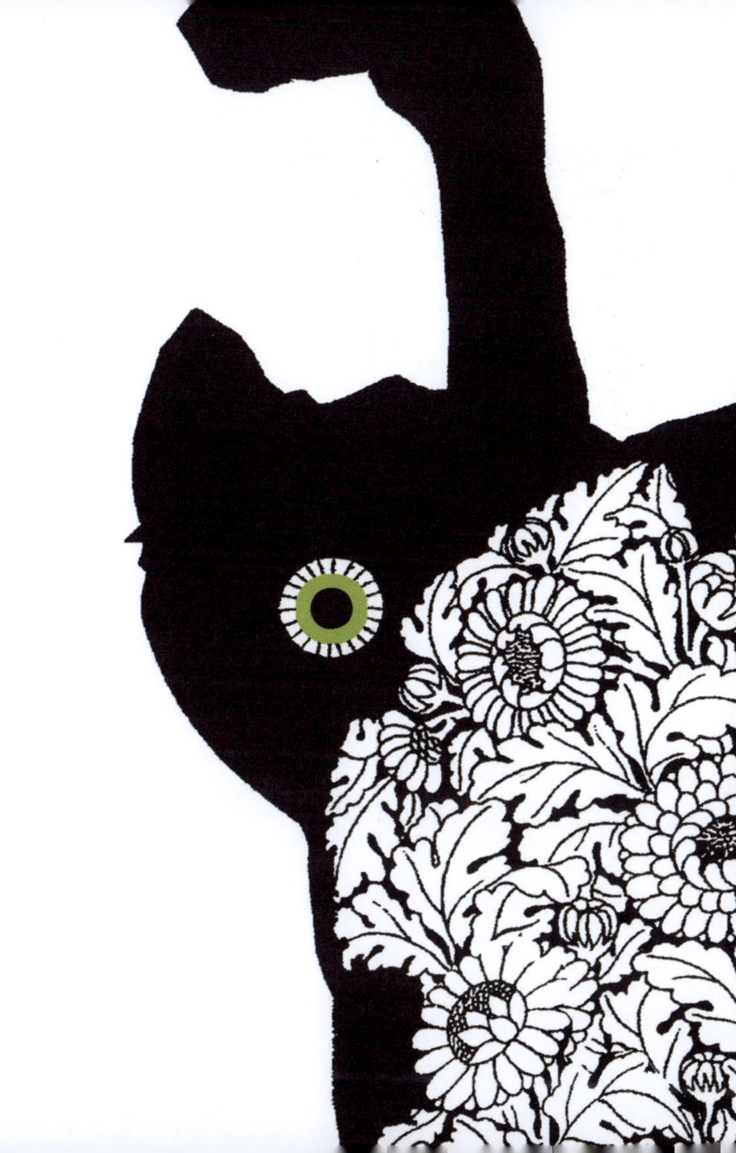

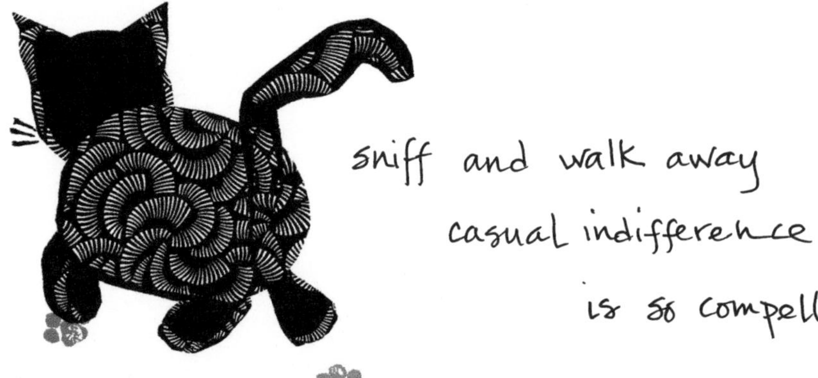

sniff and walk away
casual indifference
is so compelling

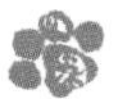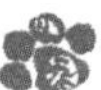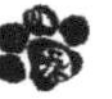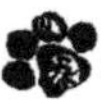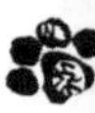

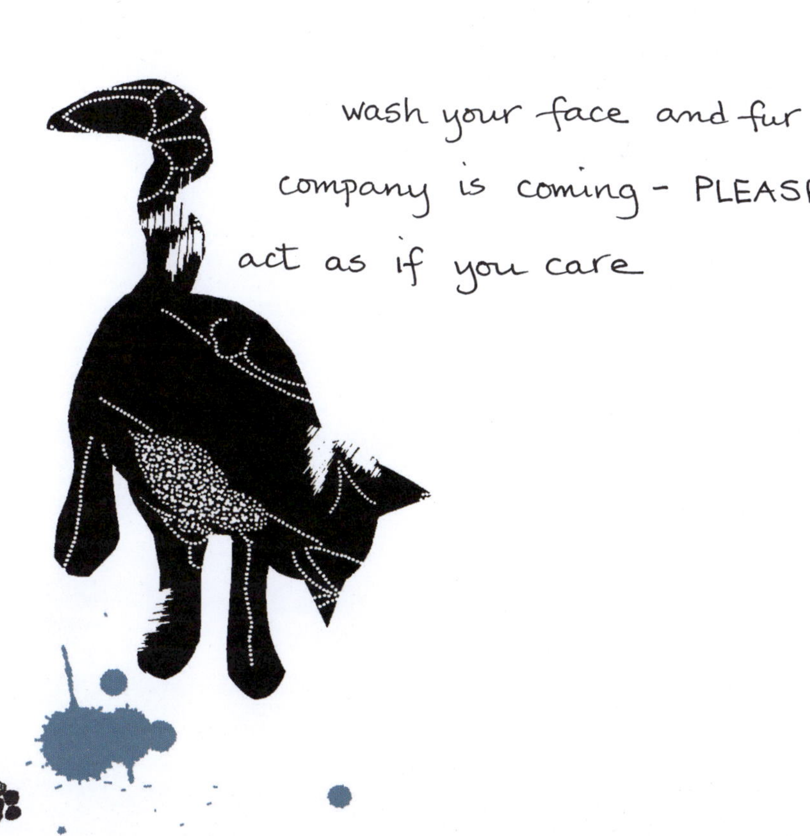

wash your face and fur
company is coming - PLEASE
act as if you care

hey there fraidy cat
ears behind the garden wall

where's the rest of you?

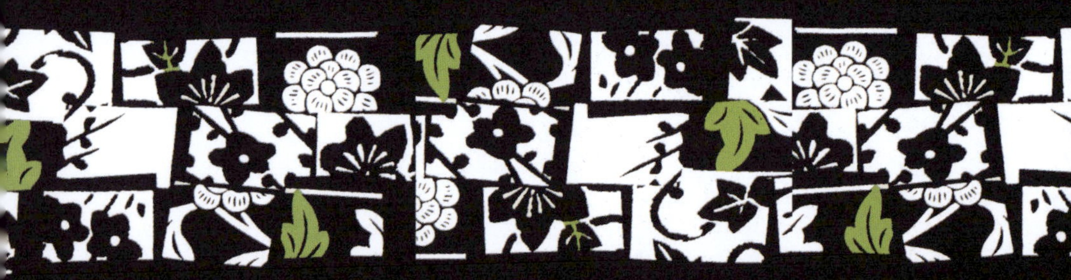

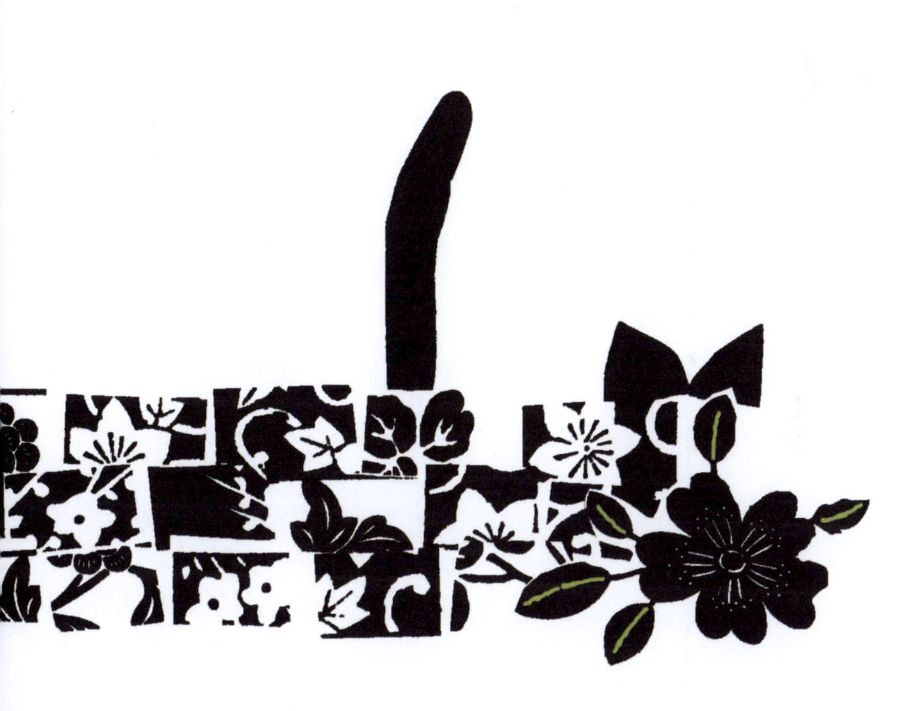

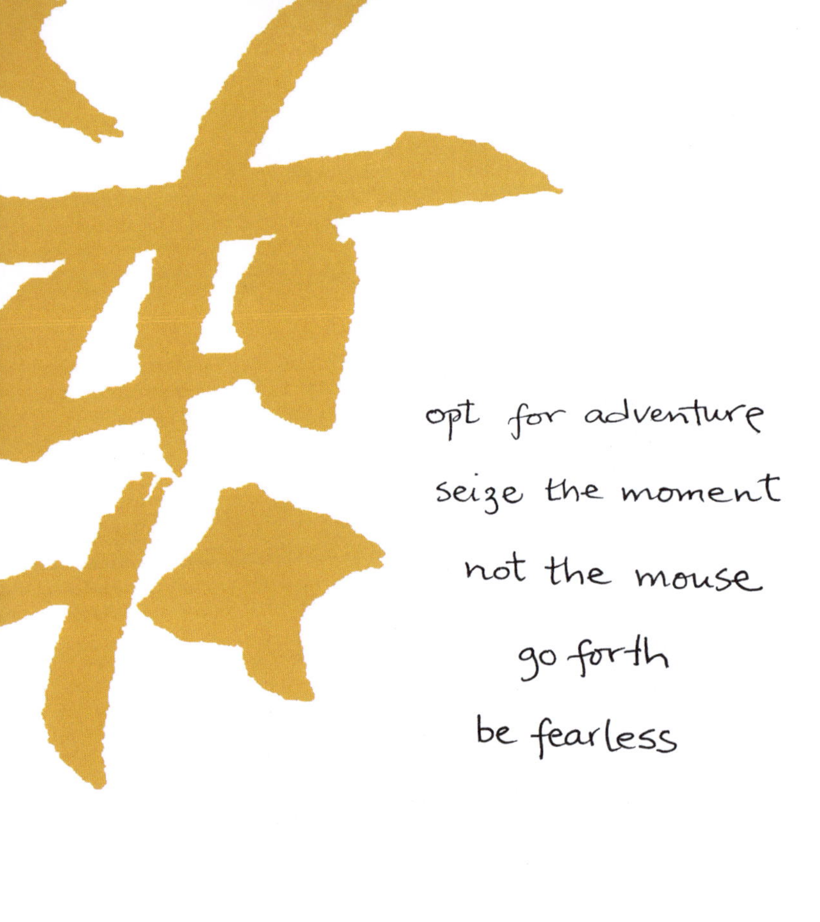

opt for adventure

seize the moment

not the mouse

go forth

be fearless

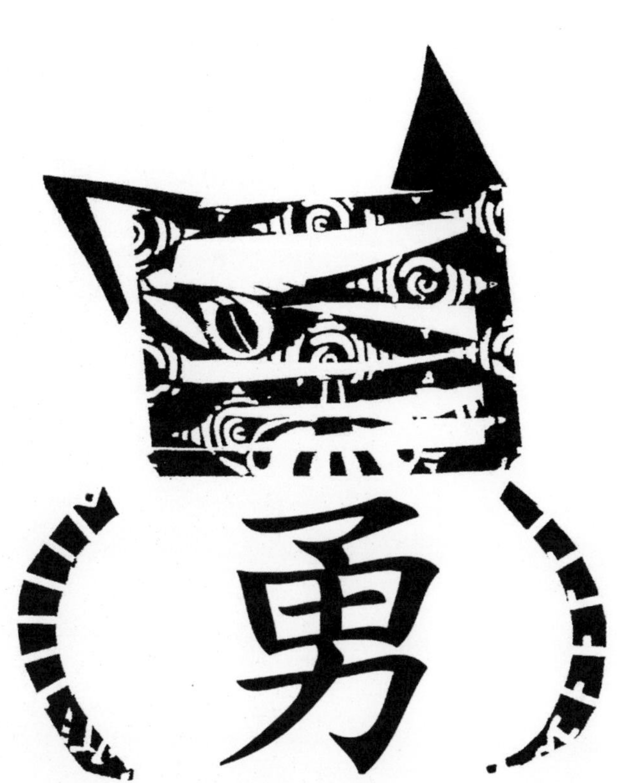

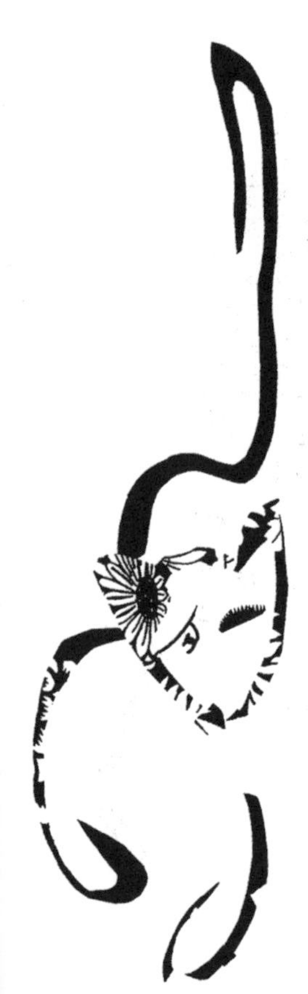

saunter through the door
glide past reproachful biped
outline your demands

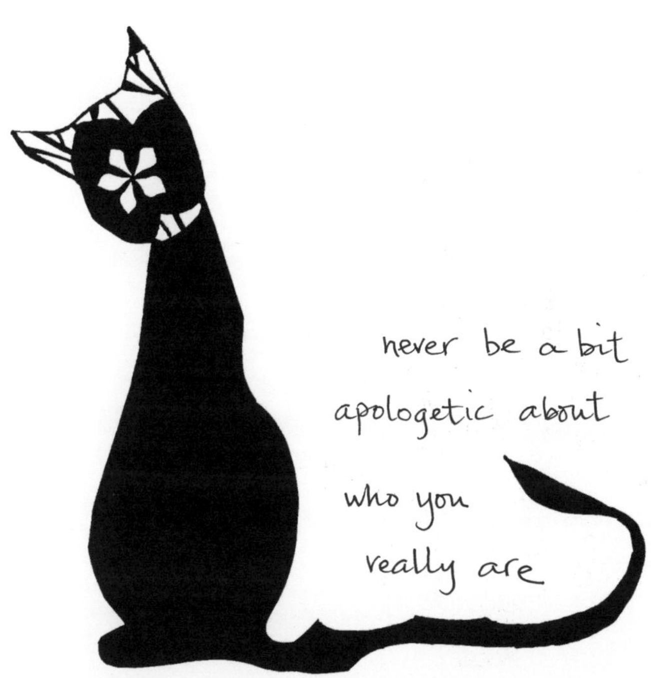
never be a bit
apologetic about
who you
really are

osmose through the fence
slip into the neighbor's yard
taunt the indoor cat

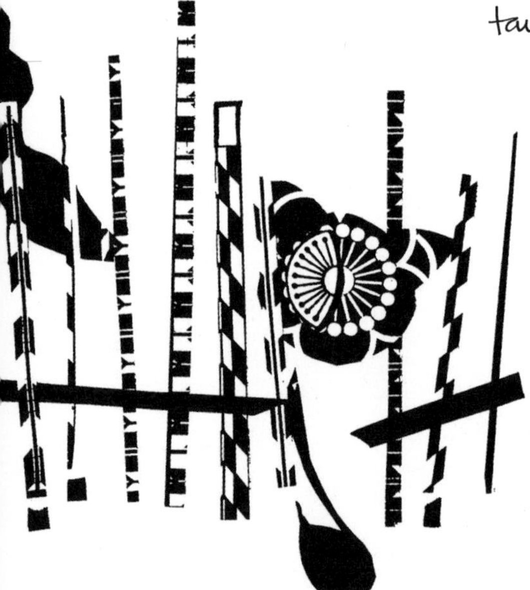

do not consider

a step in this direction

you will be sorry

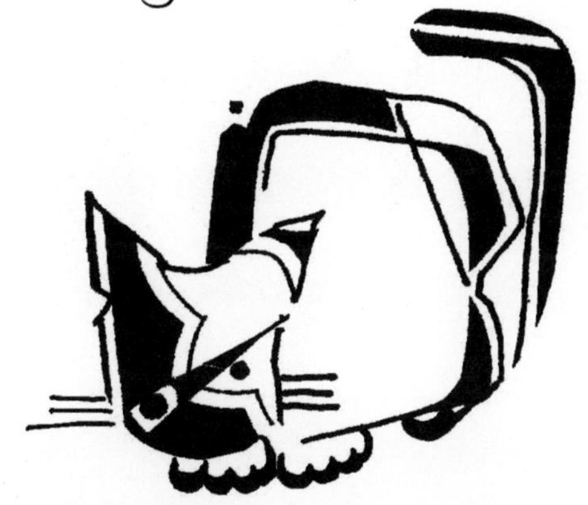

a full moon above   invitation to maraud

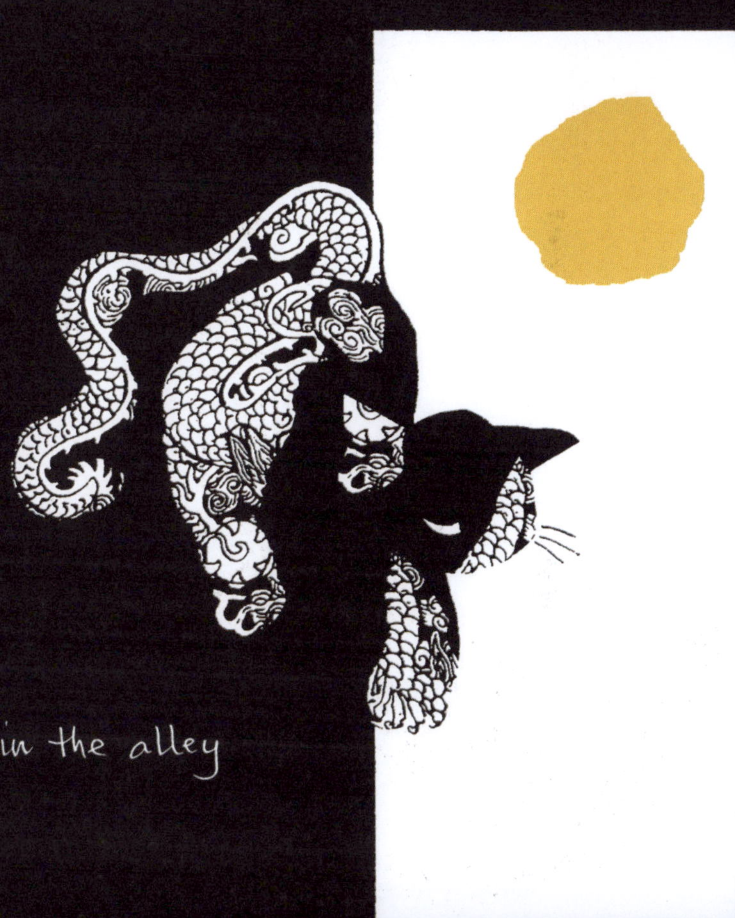
in the alley

MeOOW meeee MeeoWW
MEEoow
Meow Meow
Meow
Meow MEow
Meow Meow
MEWWW
Meoo
MEOW
MEOW
MEOW
MEOW
MEOW
MEOW MEOW
MEOW MEOW
MEOW MEOW MEOW
MEOW

be most insistent
without equivocation
ask for what you want

Meeeoooww

assail your human

be relentless and be

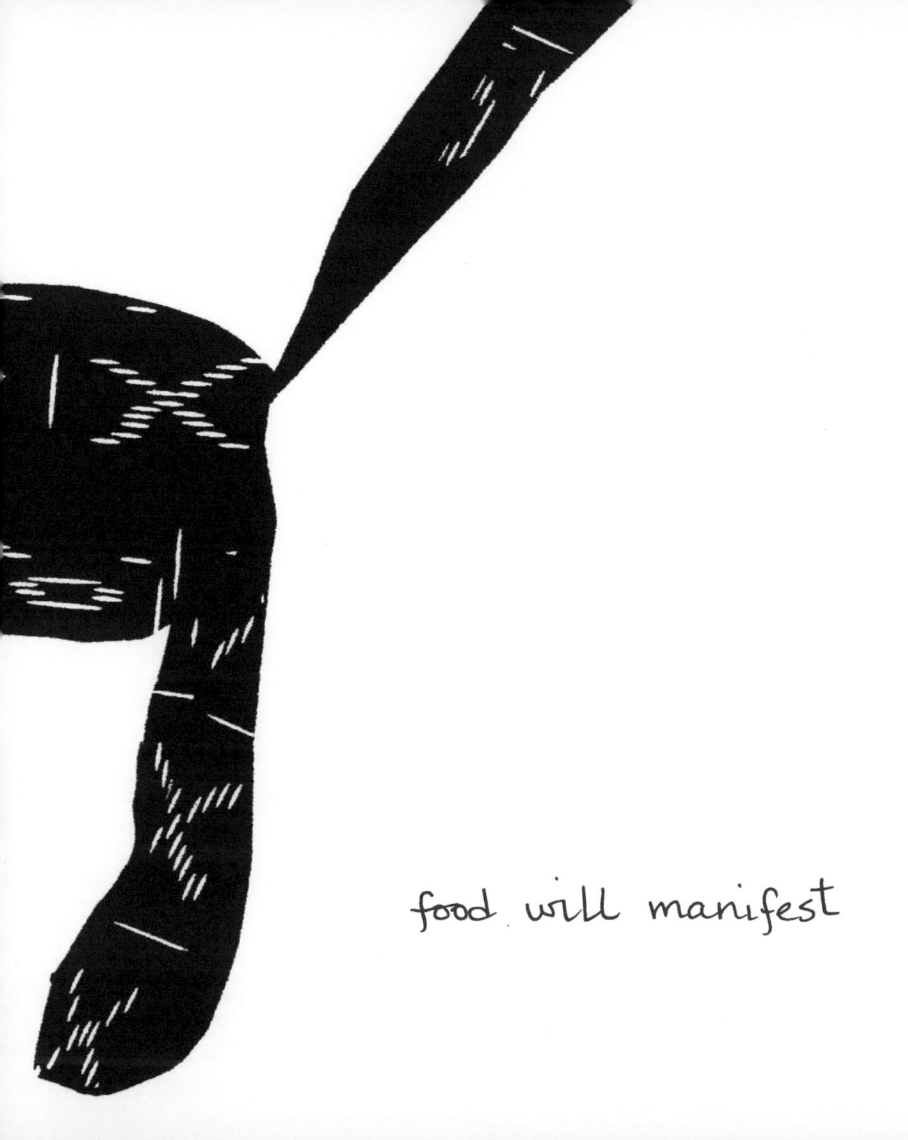
food will manifest

my heart belongs to no one
in particular

GOT FOOD ?

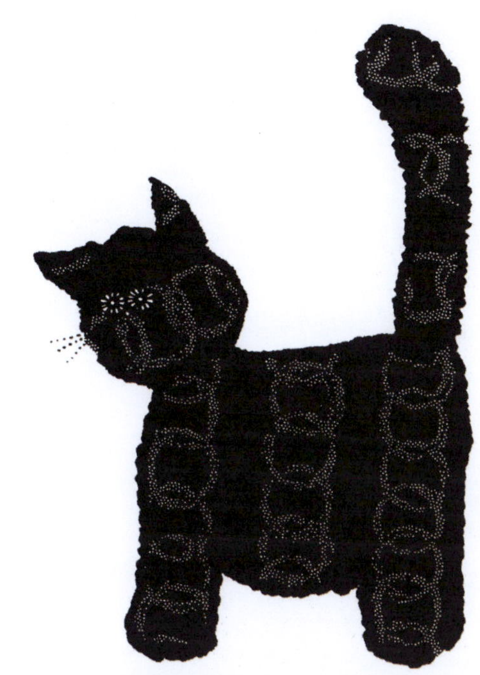
I  you

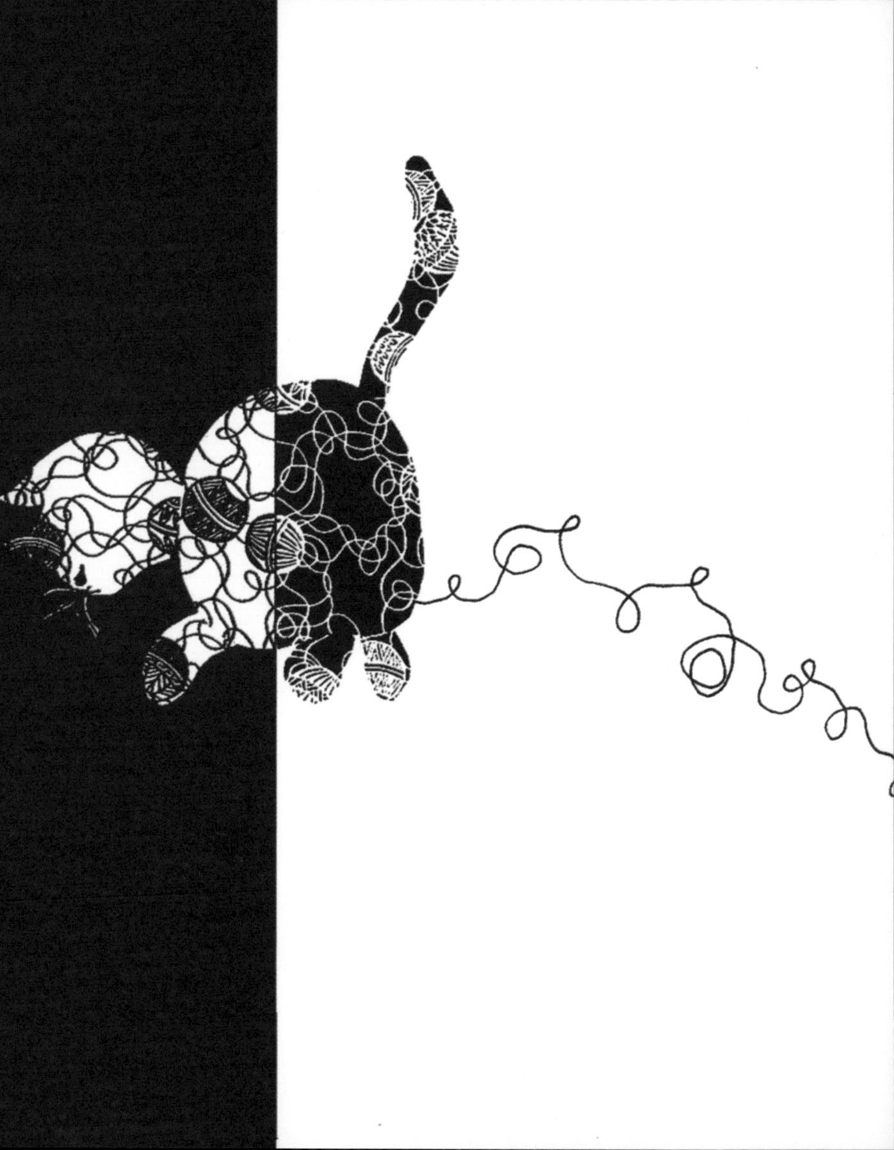

please don't bother me
something really engaging
has just replaced you

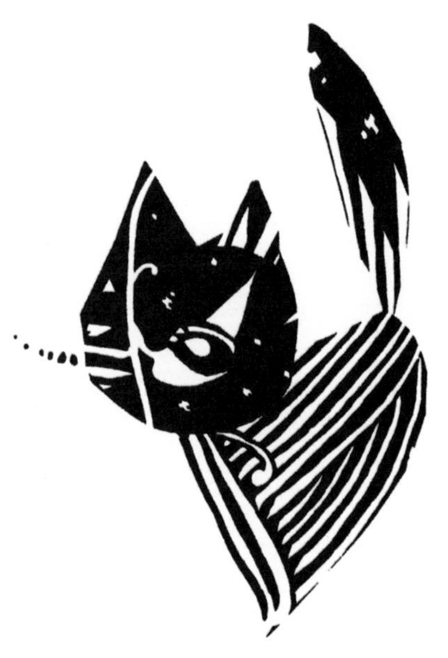

manners ? nevermind
leave those to the dinner guests
you're the centerpiece

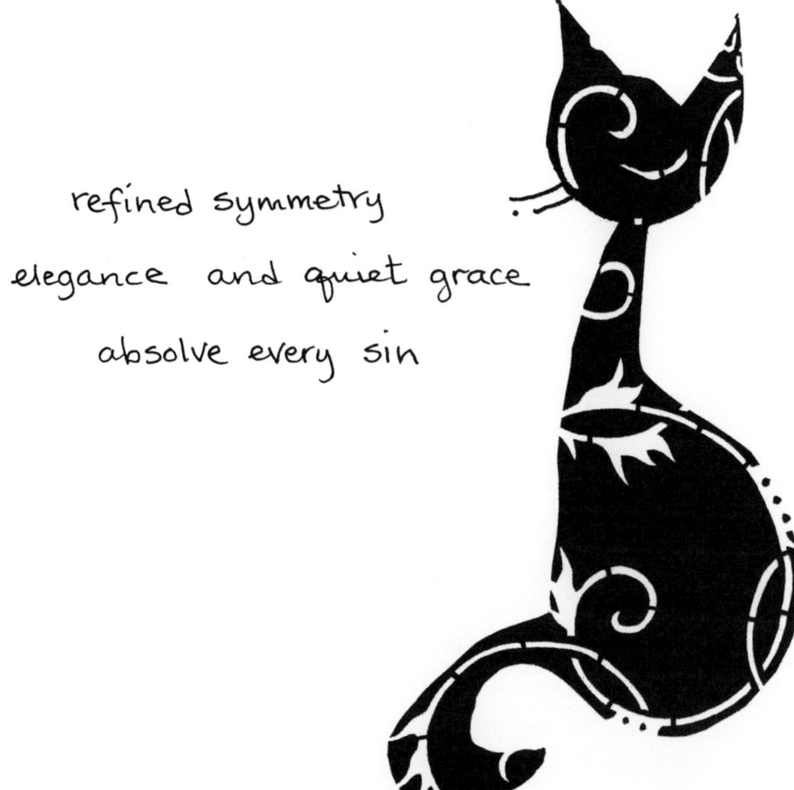
refined symmetry
elegance and quiet grace
absolve every sin

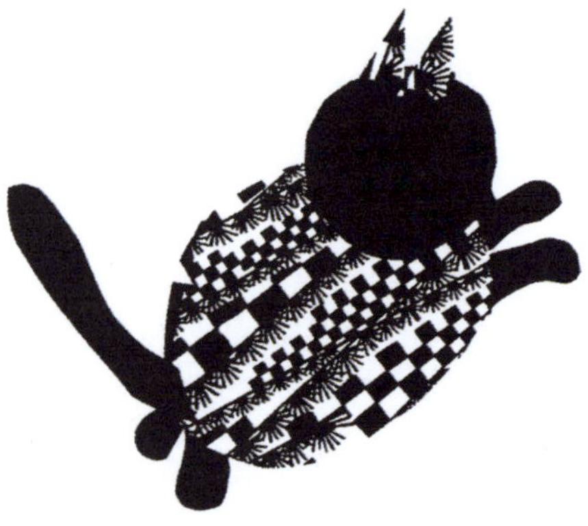
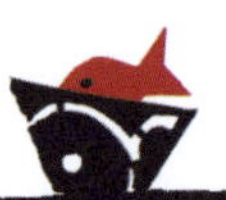
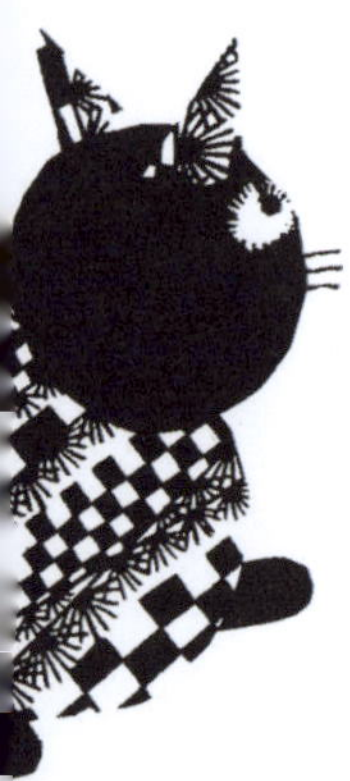

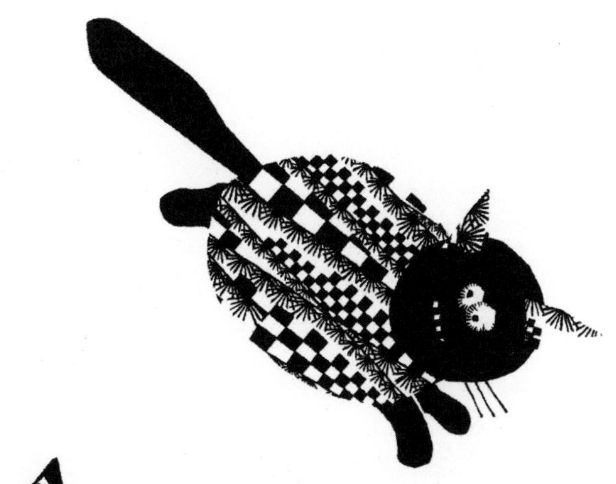
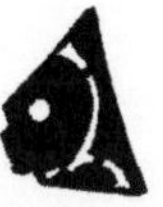

a quick perusal
single leap to counter top
mission accomplished

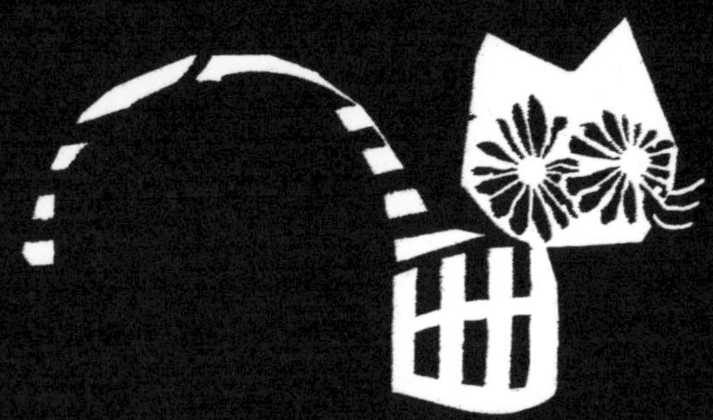

inhale now exhale

enjoy the present moment

in a blink its gone

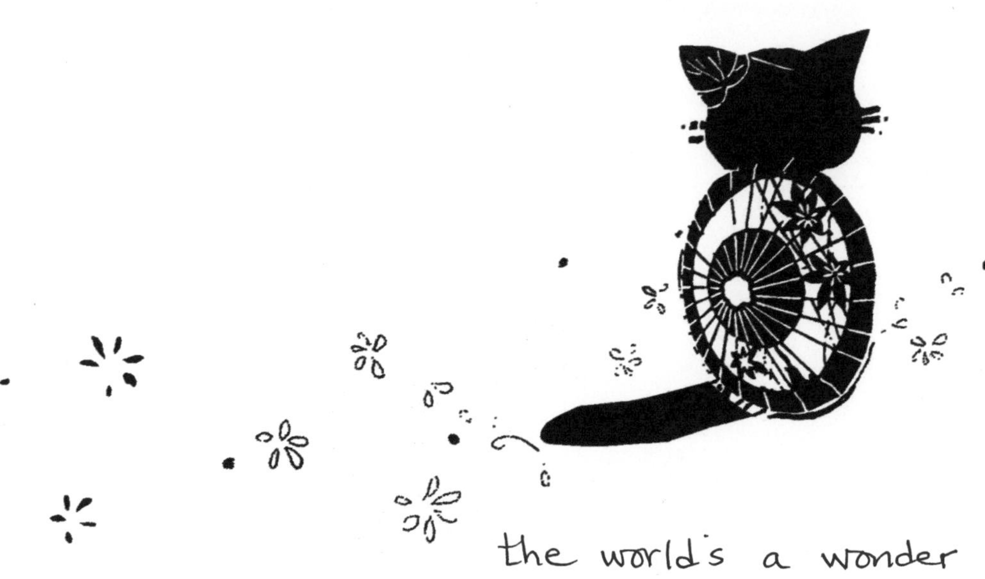

the world's a wonder
gaze for hours out the window
at life's rich pageant

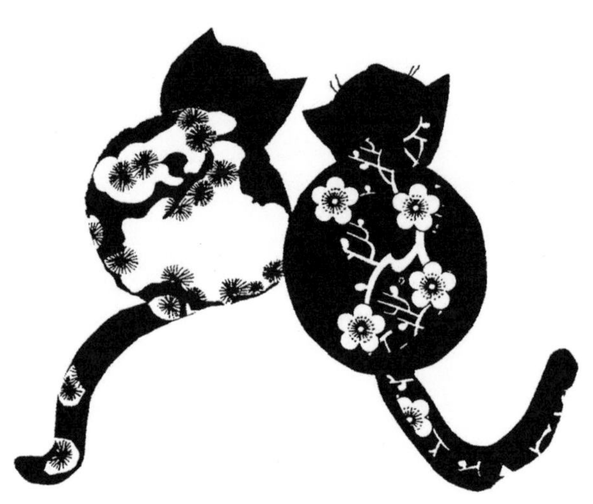

there's no substitute
for an idle afternoon
spent with a good friend

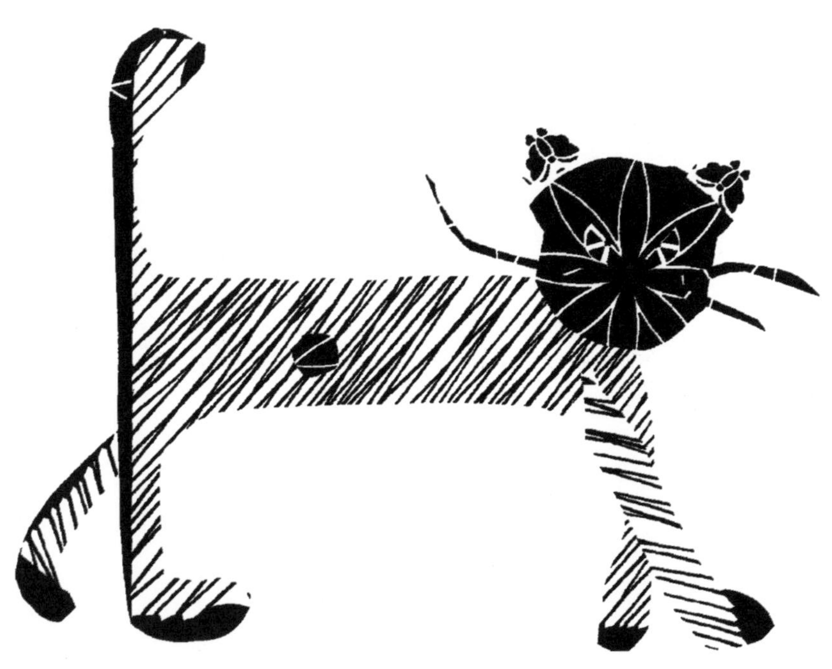

MALE SOCIOPATH
in search of co-dependent
must love fur and tails

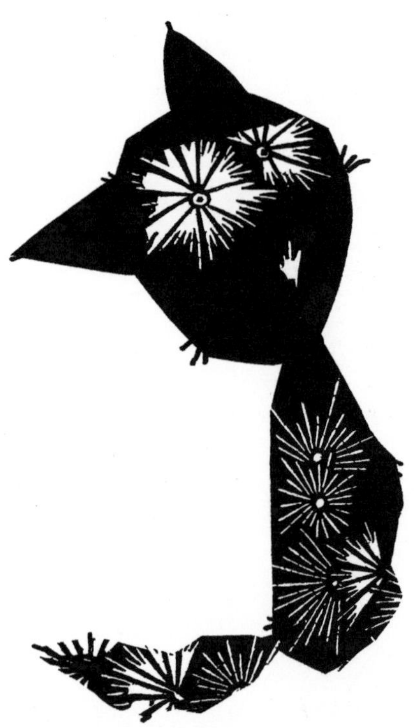

boring day until
some unexpected something
changes everything

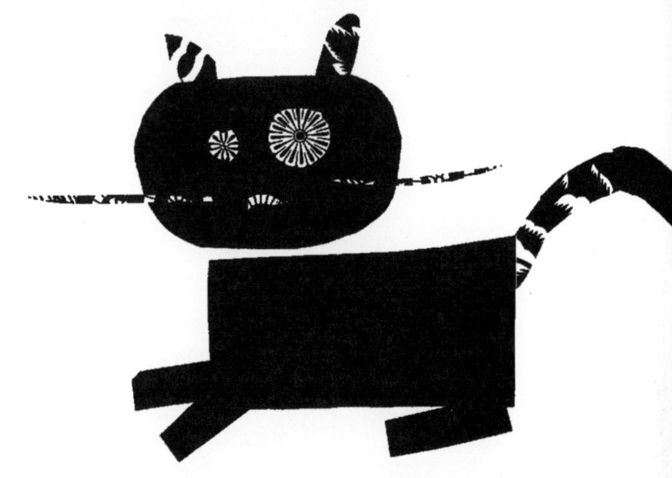

je ne sais quoi – that
special "whatever" a cat
brings to the party

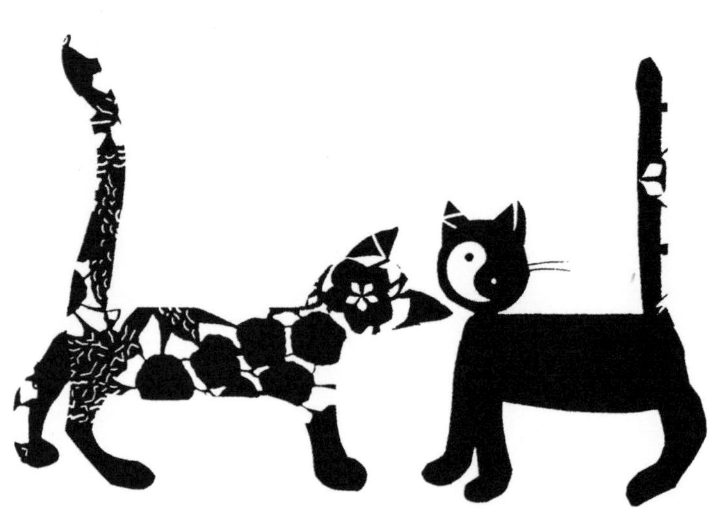

what perfect balance
yin of purr ☯ yang of YEOW
the tao of kitties

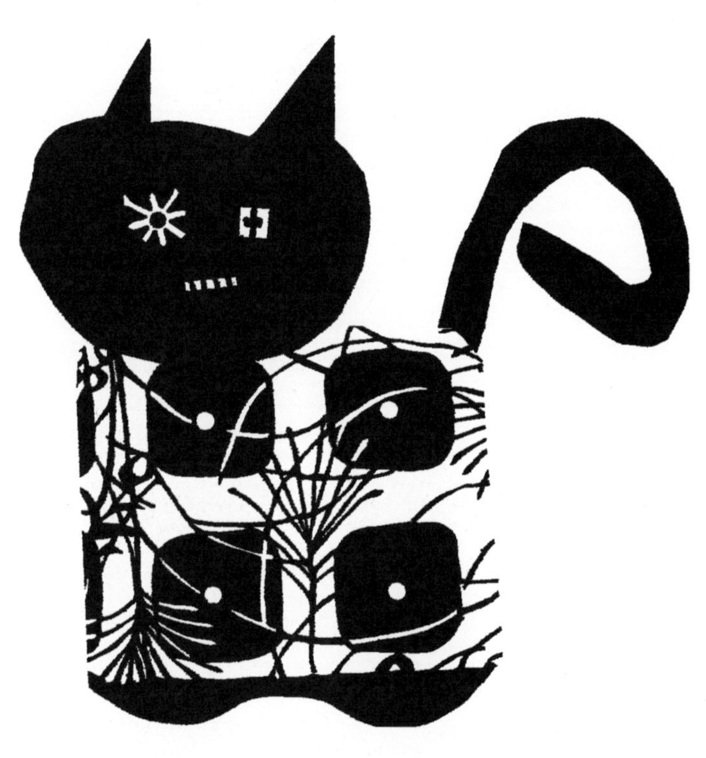

Crazed, catatonic
neurotic or psychotic

Ordinary cat.

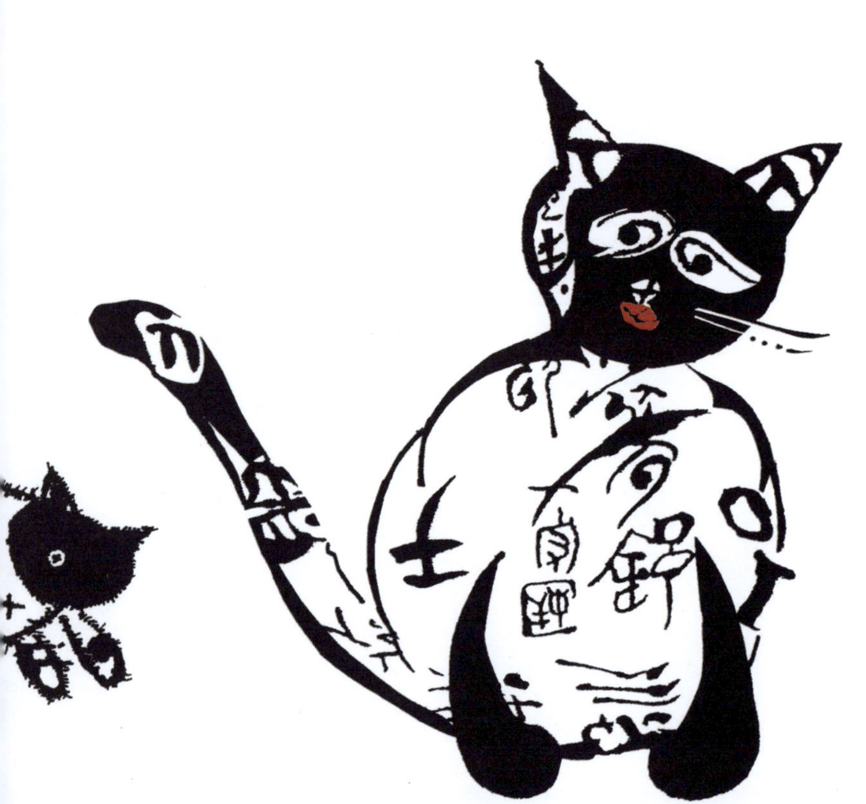

newborn kittens

for six spectacular weeks

the circus is in town

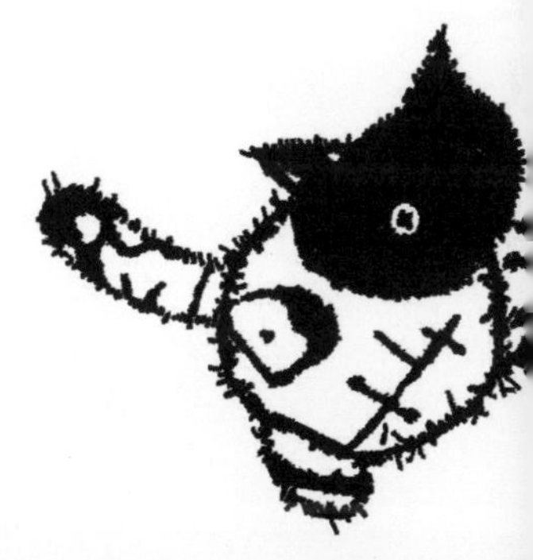

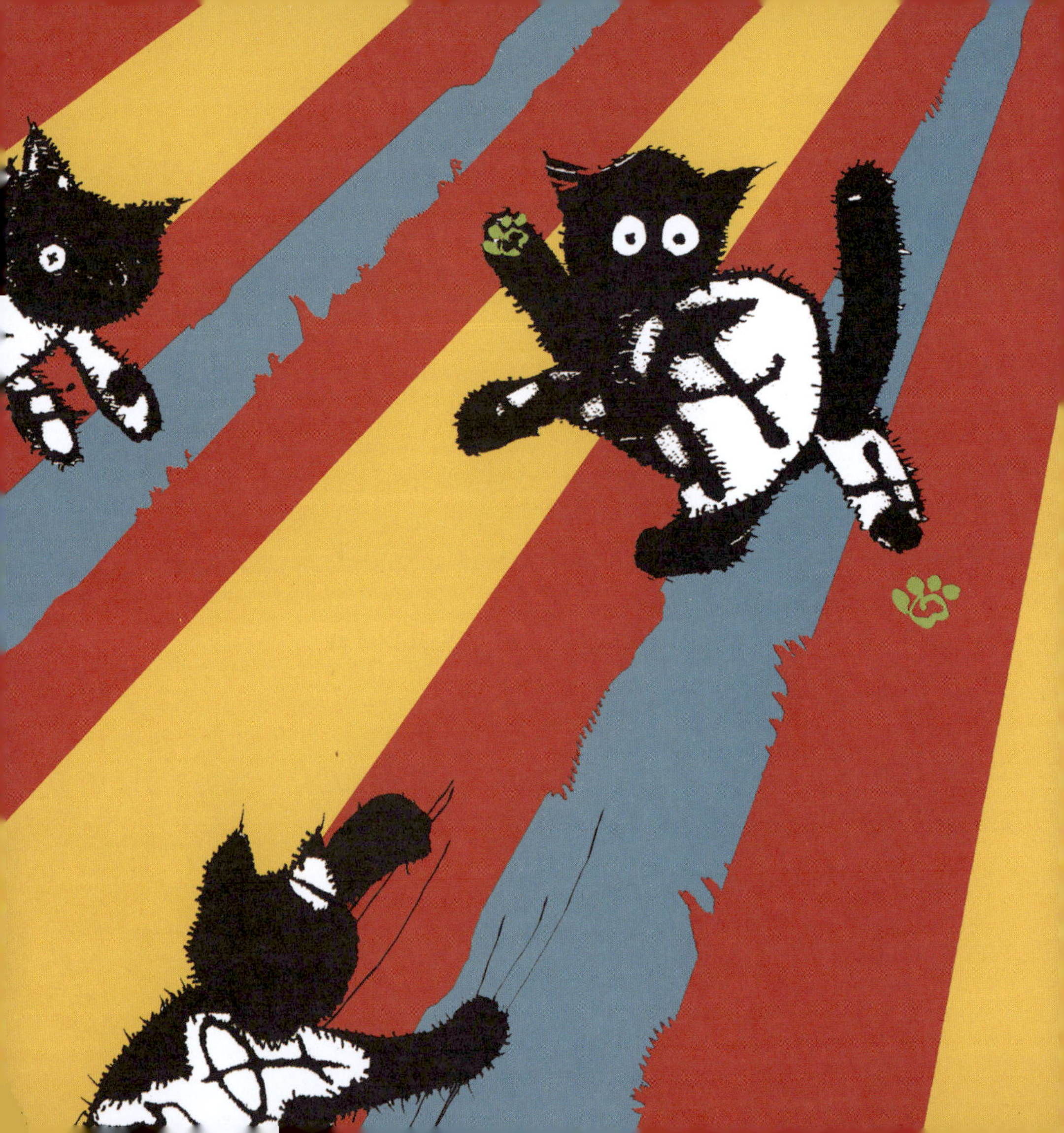

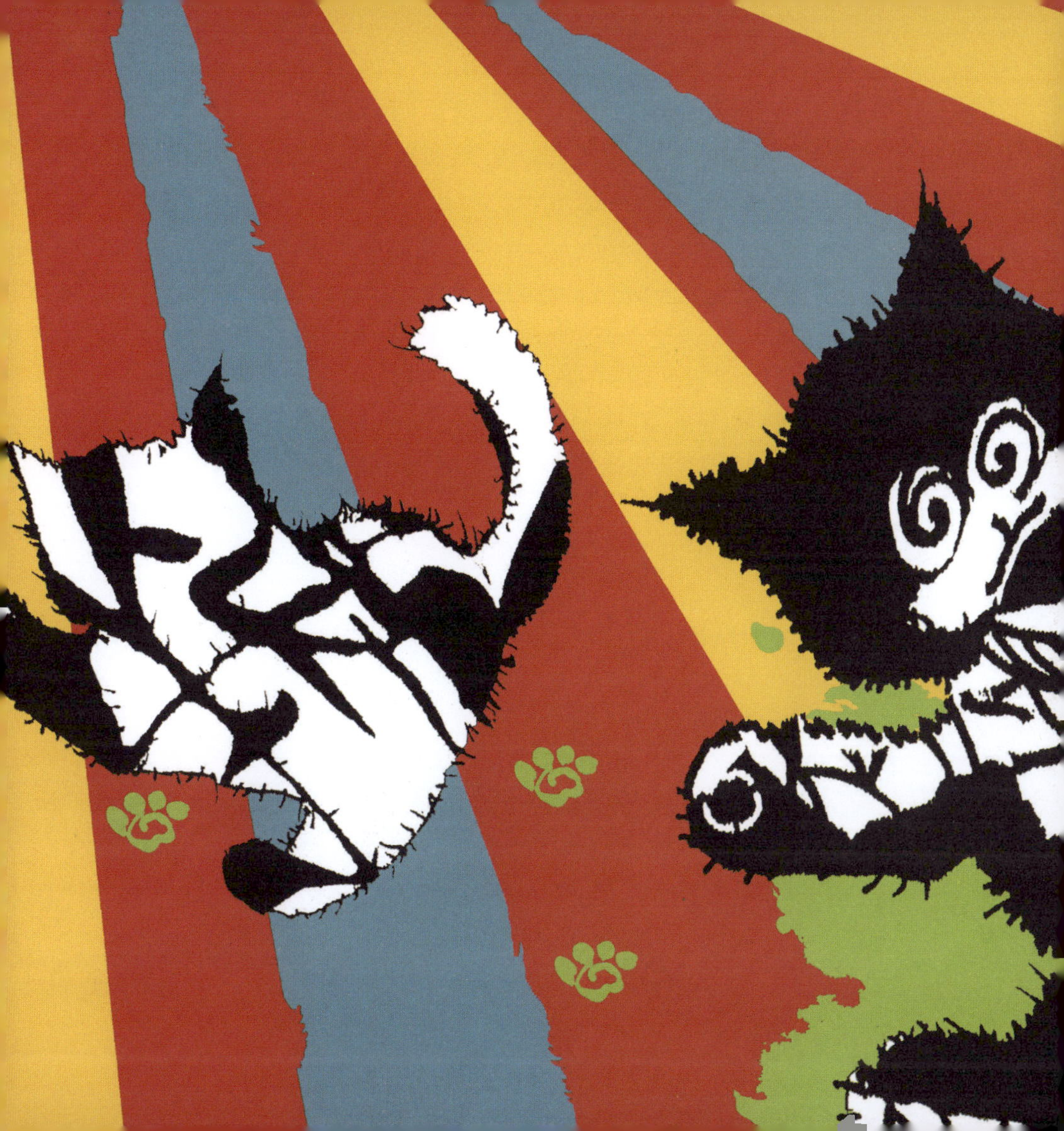

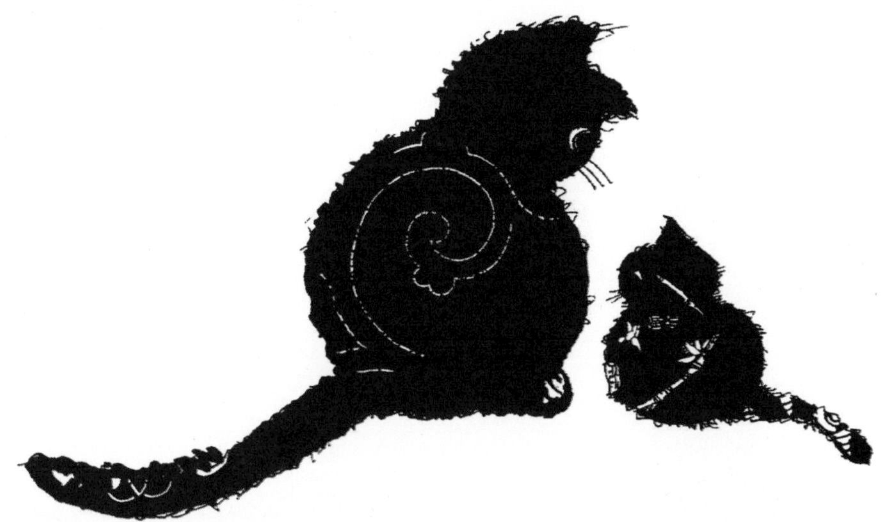
don't play in the street
never talk to strangers   and
keep those whiskers clean

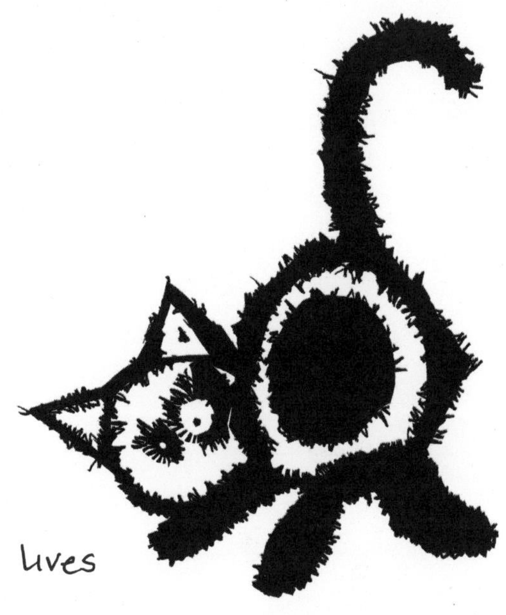

you've only nine lives
don't squander even one on
trying to behave

POETIC LICENSE

deviance from
standard form
just to serve
a point

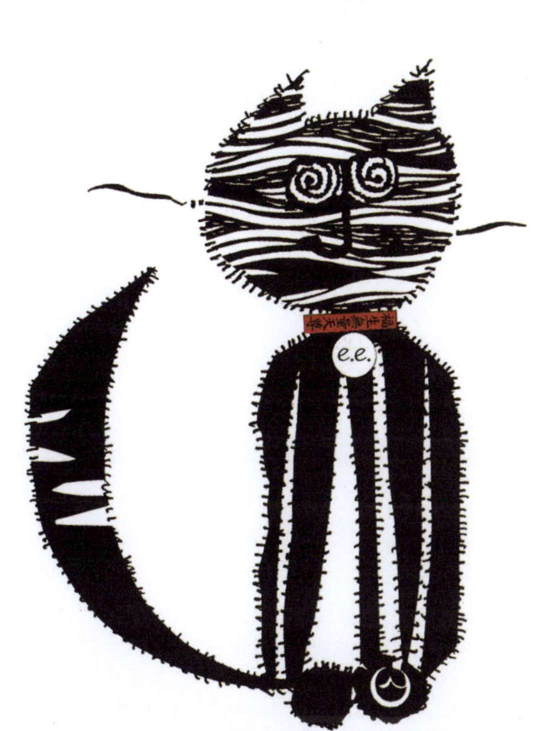
e.e.

escape

disappear

when she's completely

FRANTIC

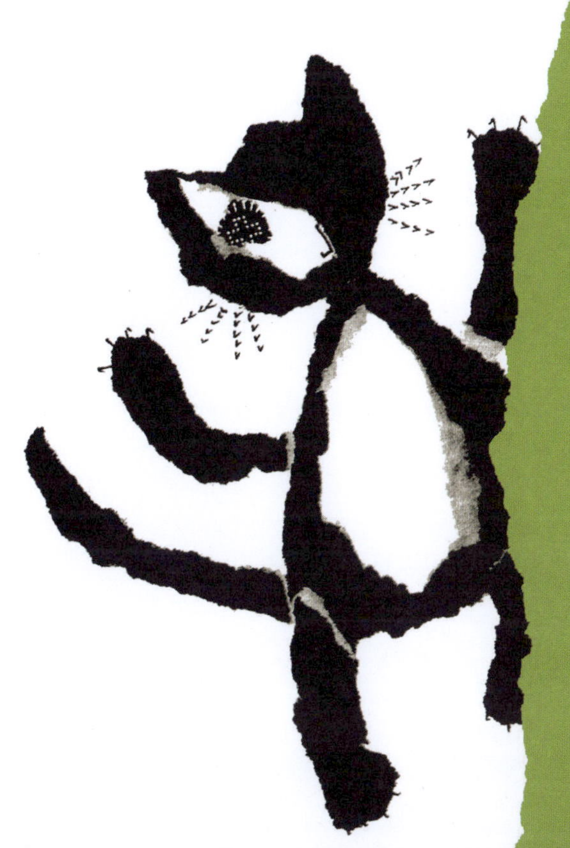

materialize

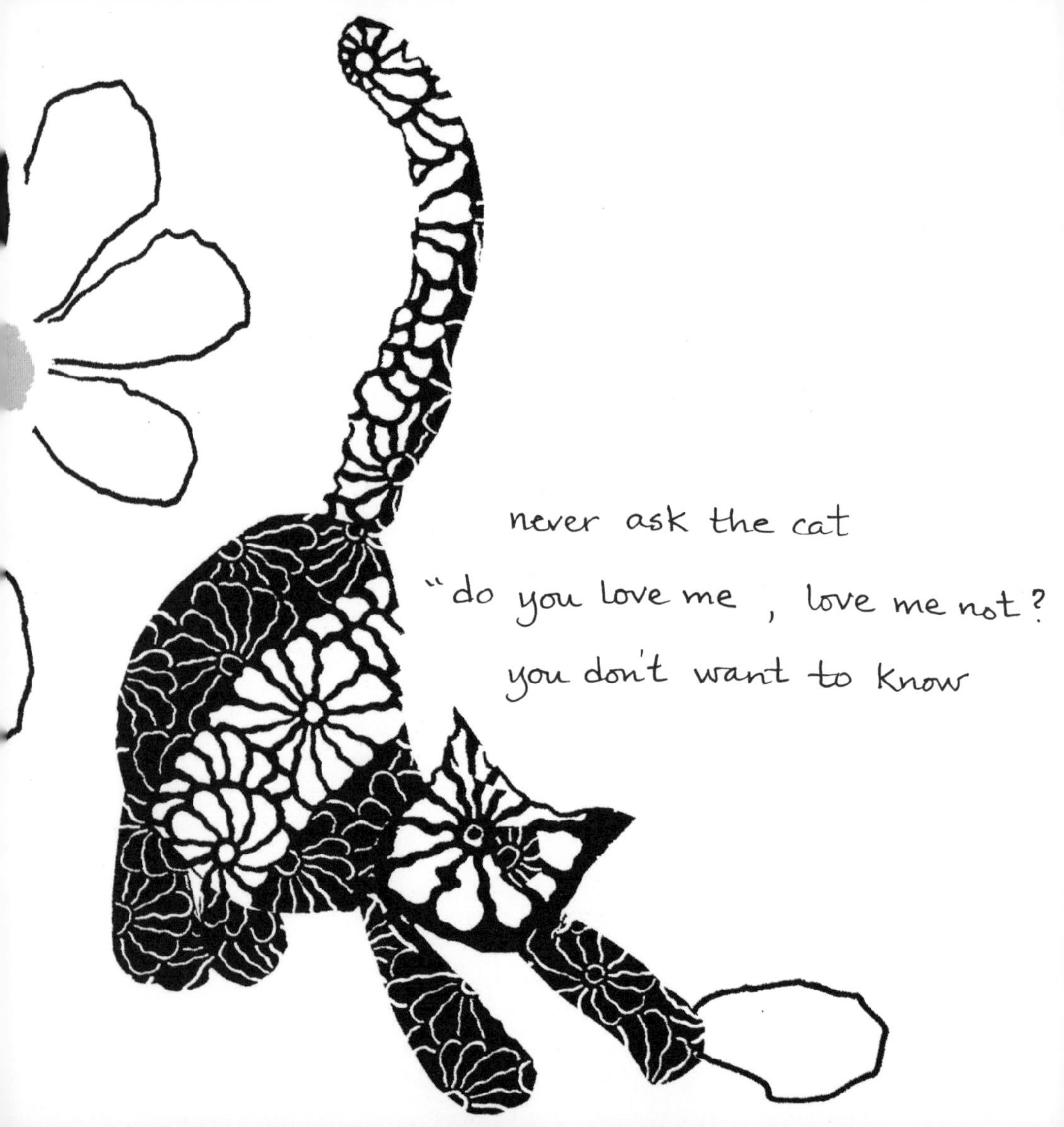
never ask the cat
"do you love me , love me not ?
you don't want to know

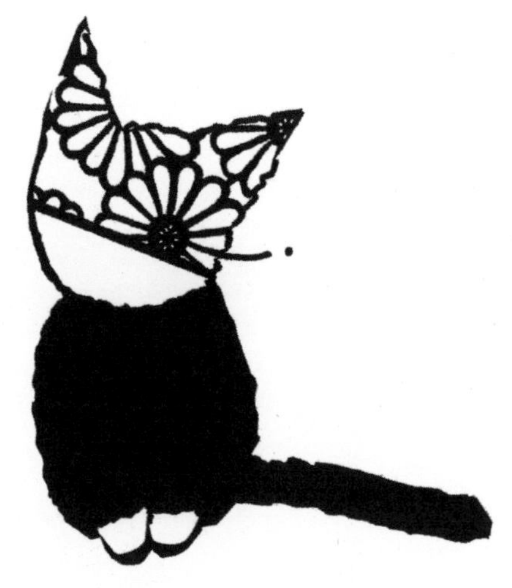

what lies behind you ?
before you?   small matters if
the cat's beside you

the subtle art of
saying thanks: a stare a blink
a well-placed hairball

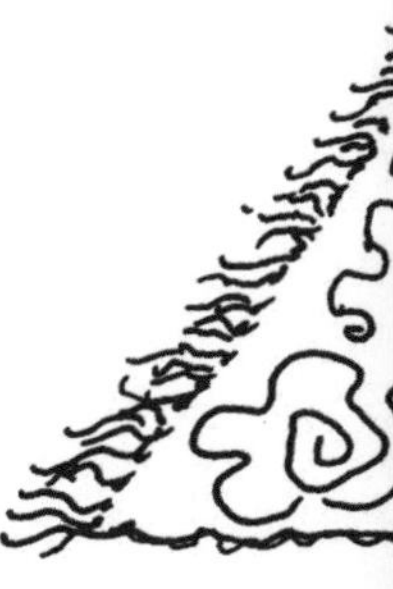

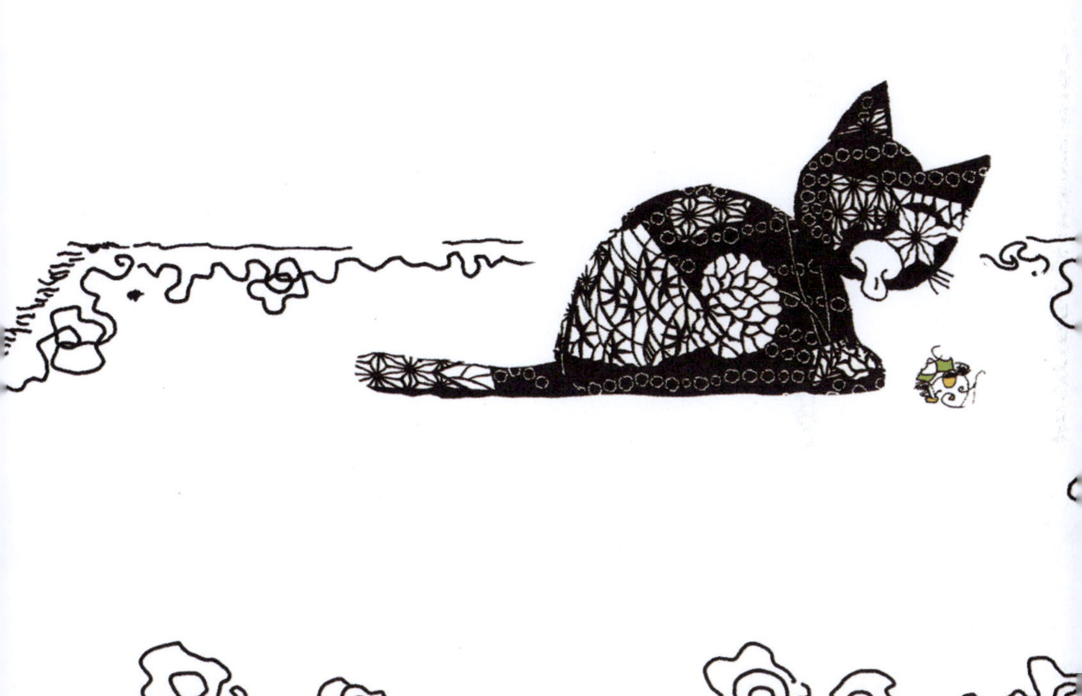

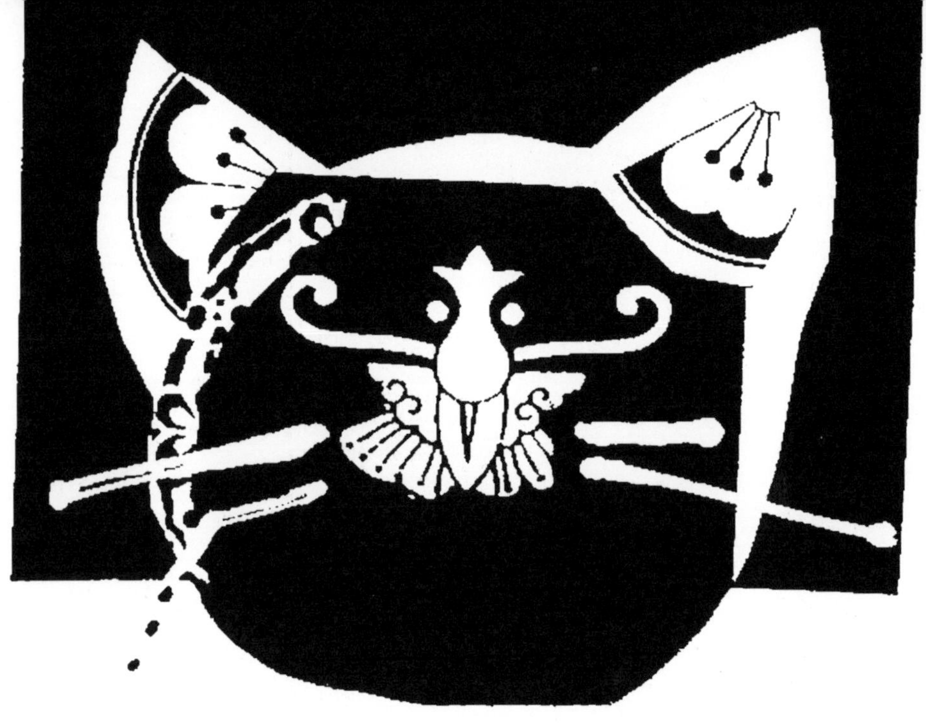

the price of freedom
eternal vigilance — wait
for the open door

just exercising

my second amendment rights :

The Bite to Bare Arms

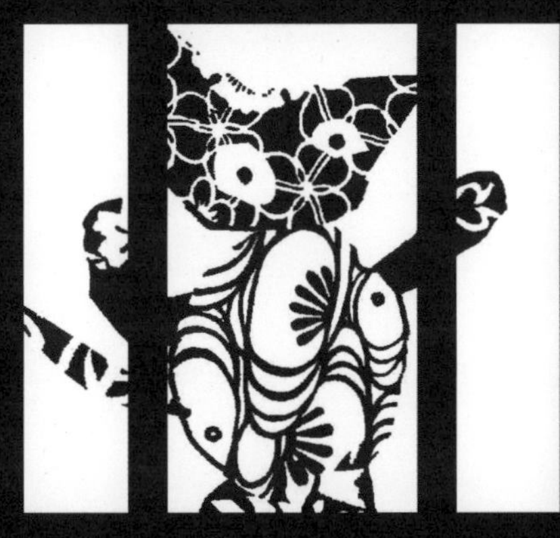

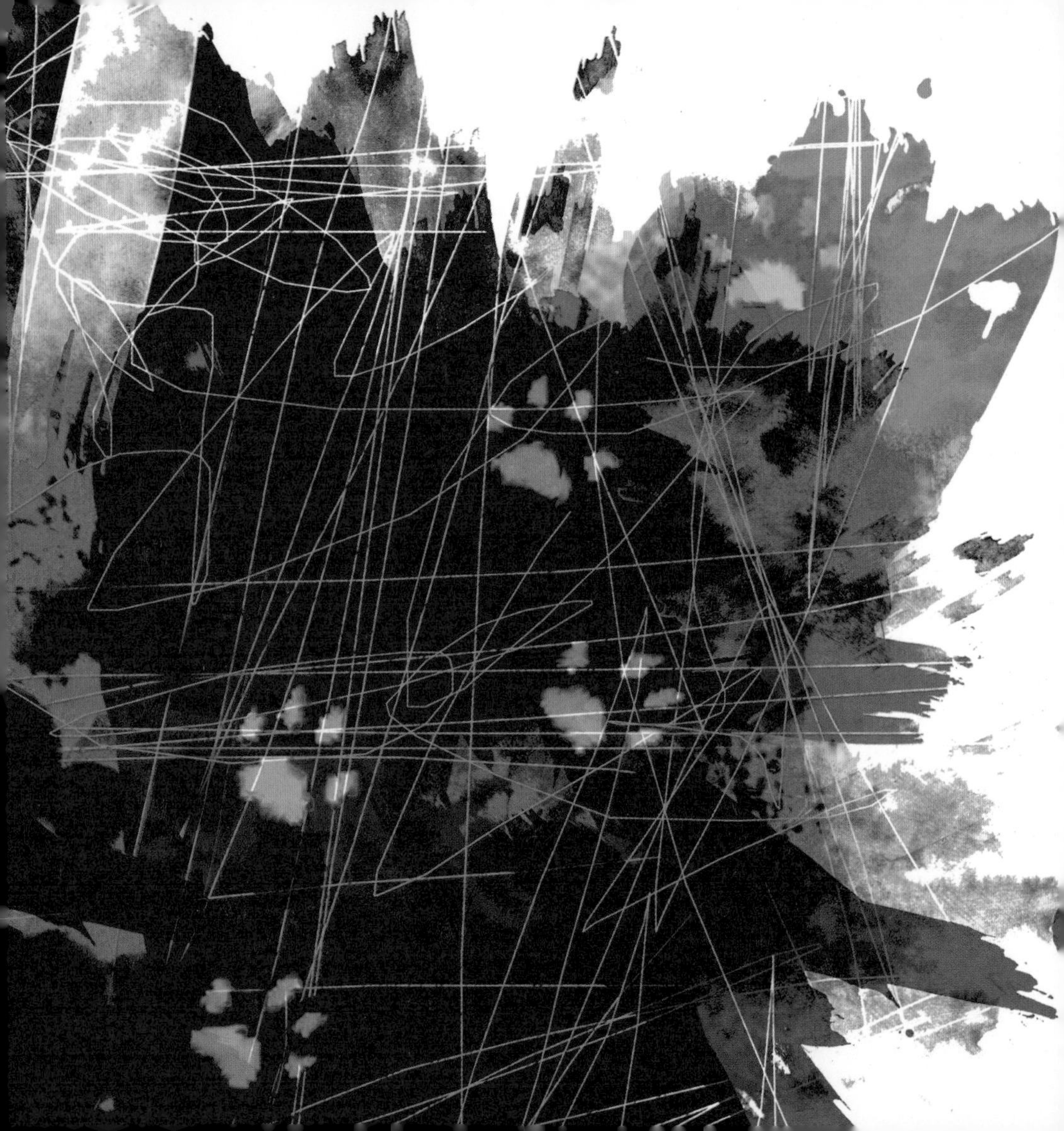

DON'T annoy the cat
he's very accomplished at
showing displeasure

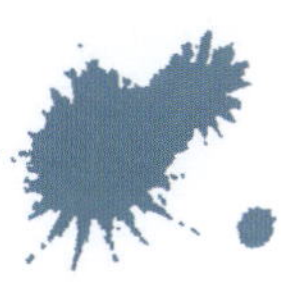

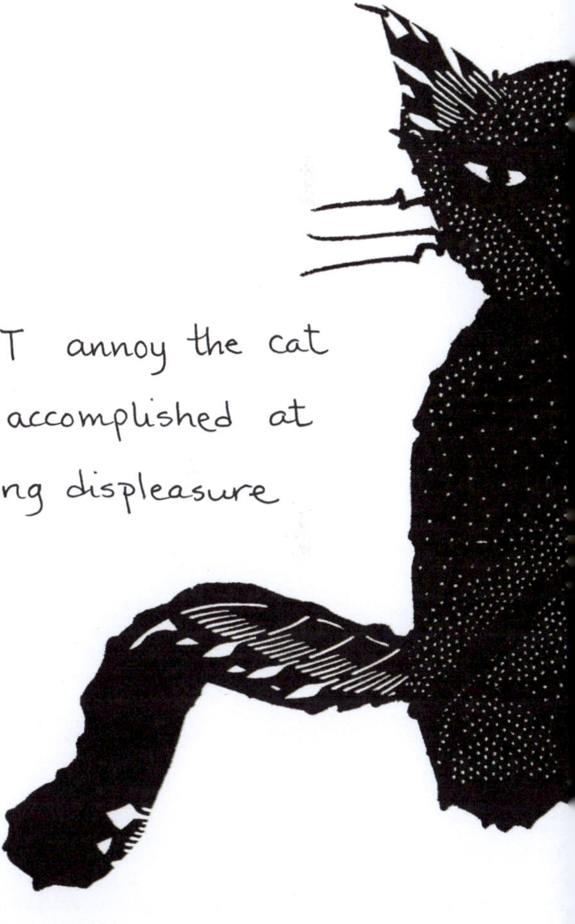

tattoos on your arms
etchings on the furniture

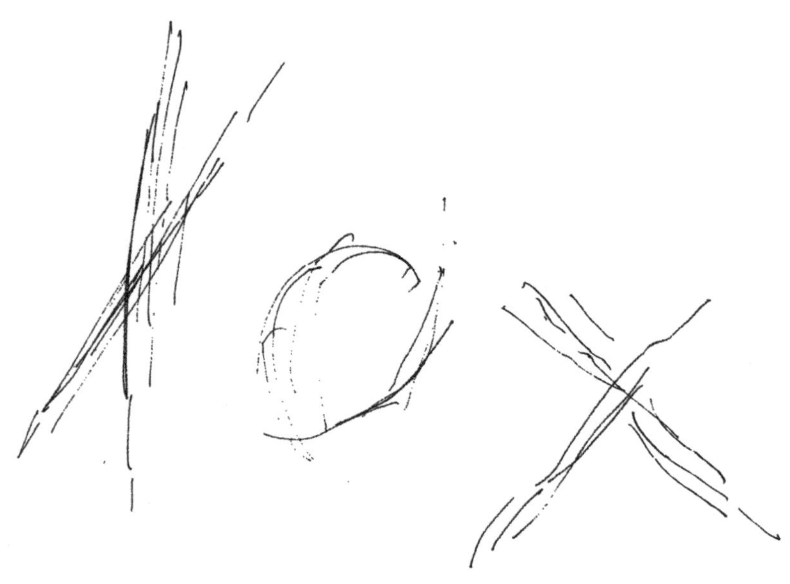

this cat's an artist

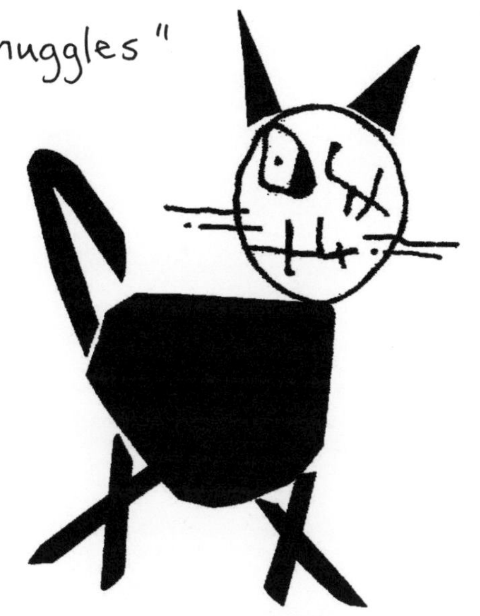

what did you expect?
of course I'm a lunatic ...
you named me
" Snuggles "

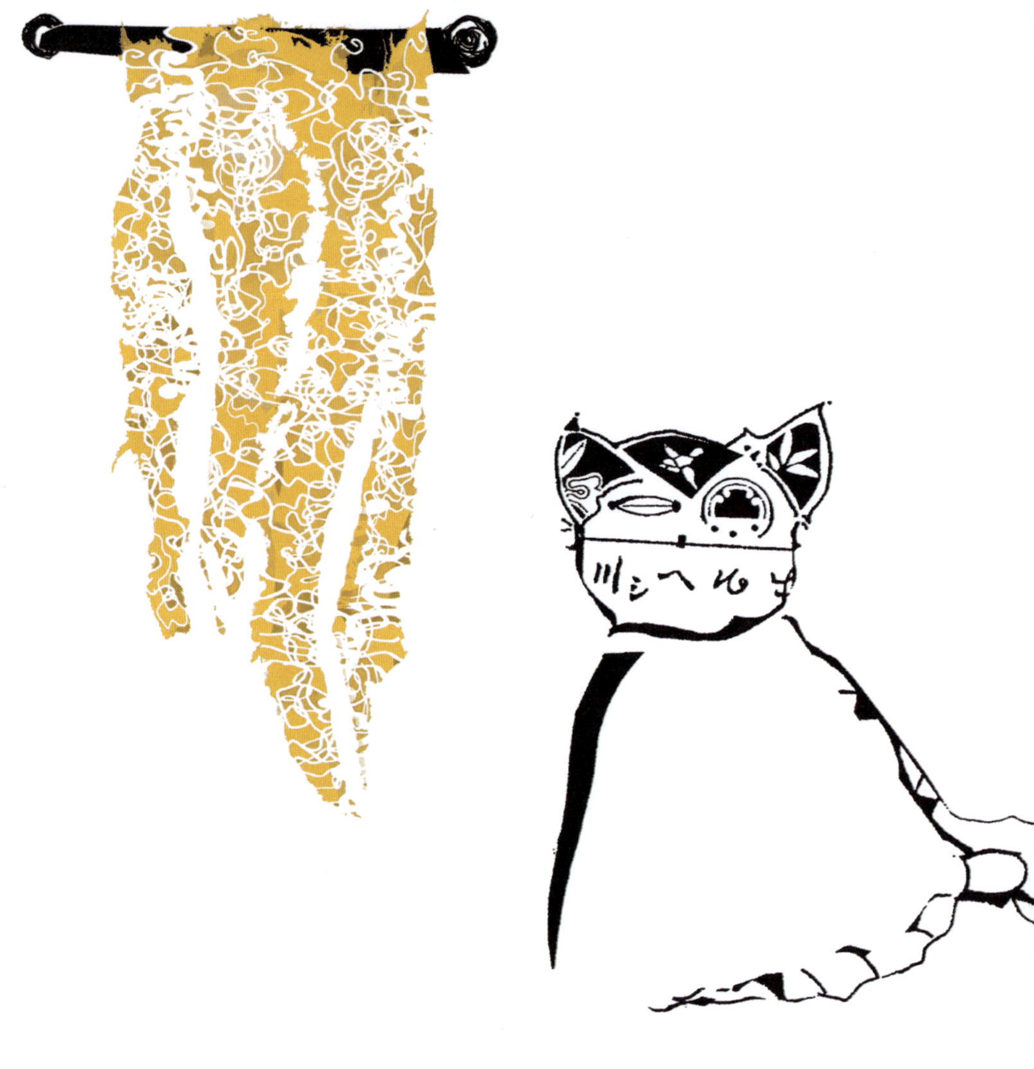

terrorize the dog

then shred the couch

and curtains

be unrepentent

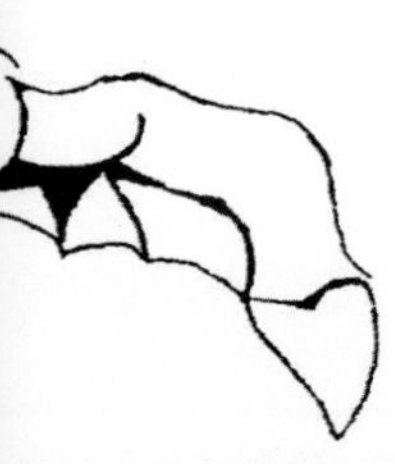

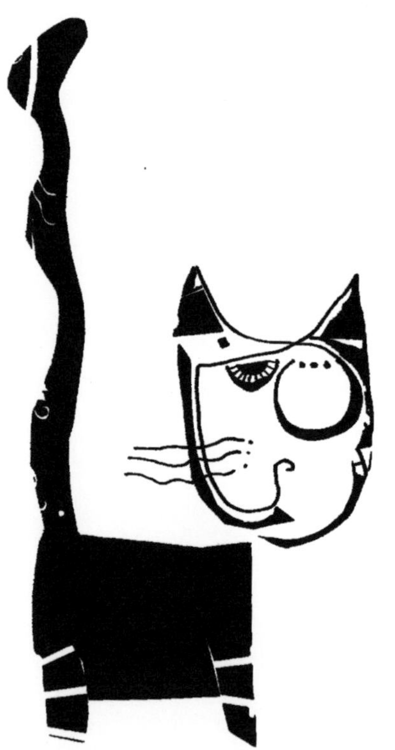

improvise a bit

life's an opportunity

to be a jazz cat

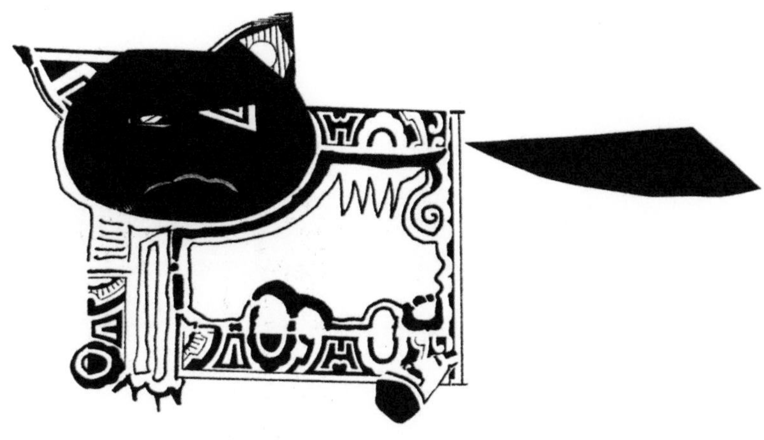

gluttony and sloth

plus those other deadly sins...

life's so bad it's good

life's a holiday
one spectacular party
wear a tuxedo

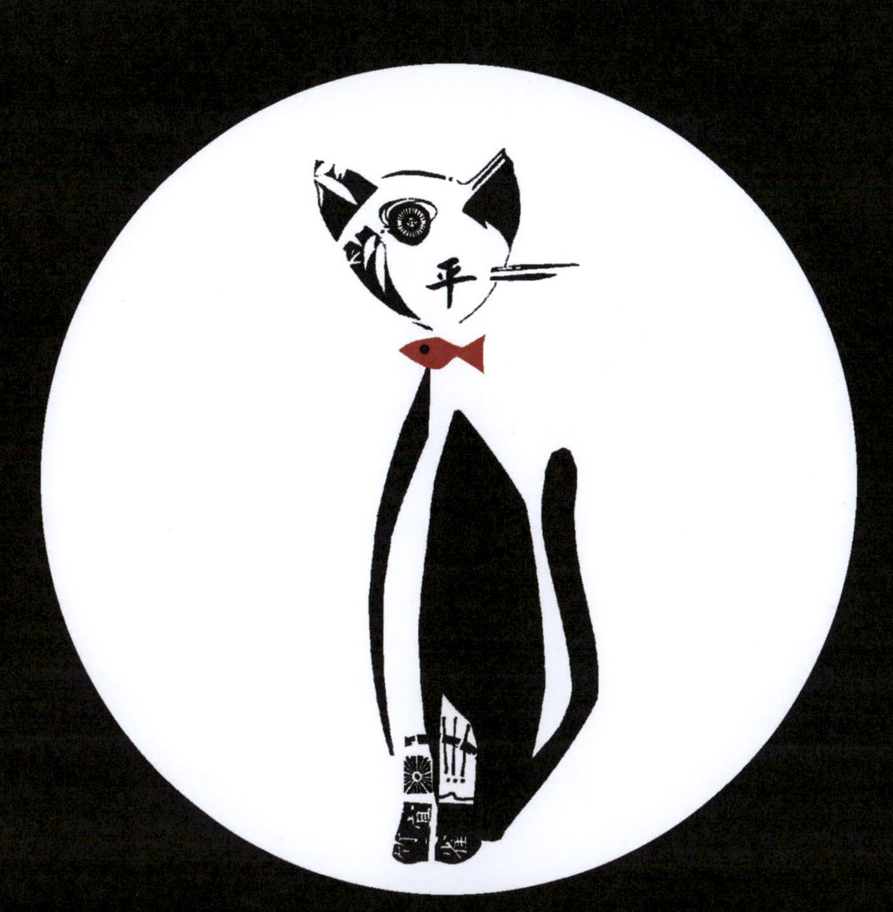

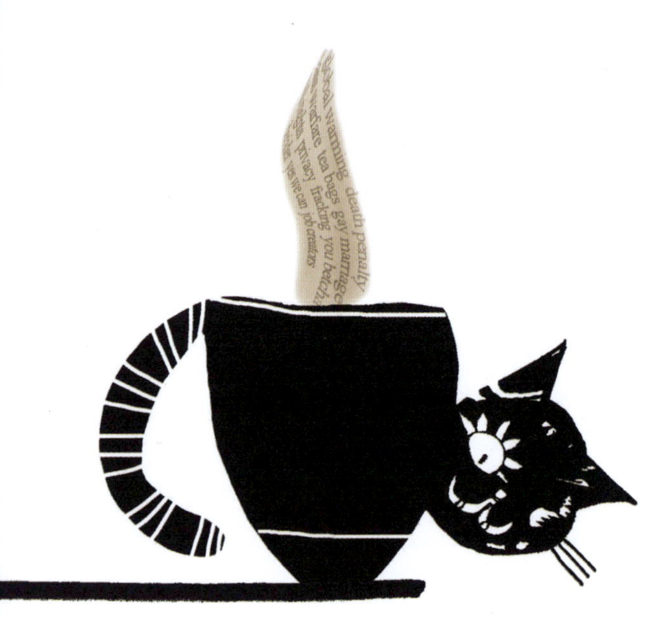

let the day begin
cup of coffee and the cat
make the news seem good

mmmm

sweet indulgence
caresses, fancy feasts, naps
cats know how to live

filling space in a
beautiful way — the fine art
of being feline

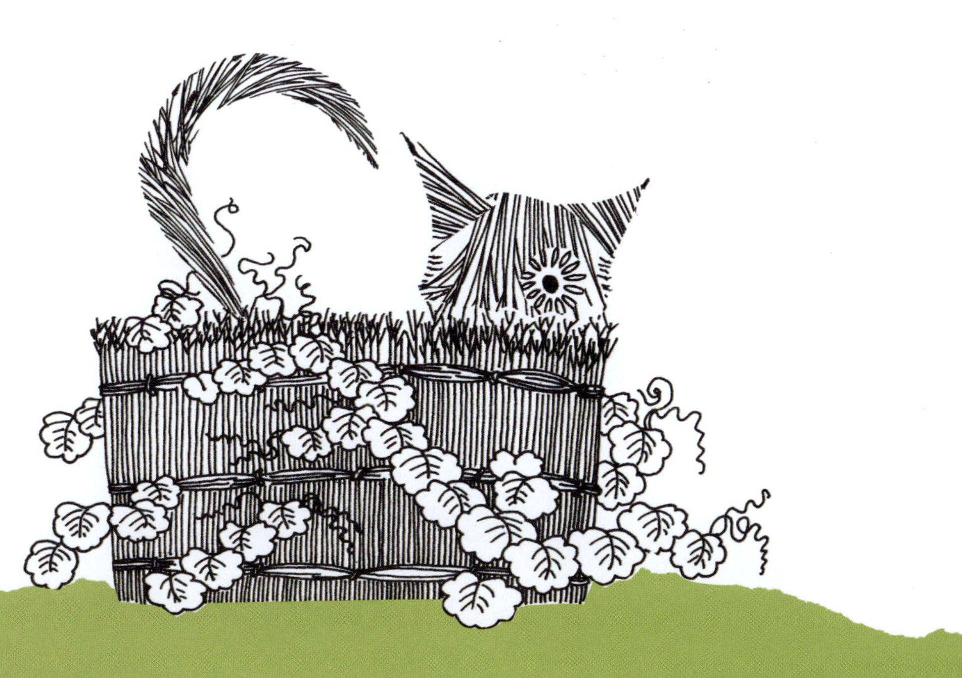

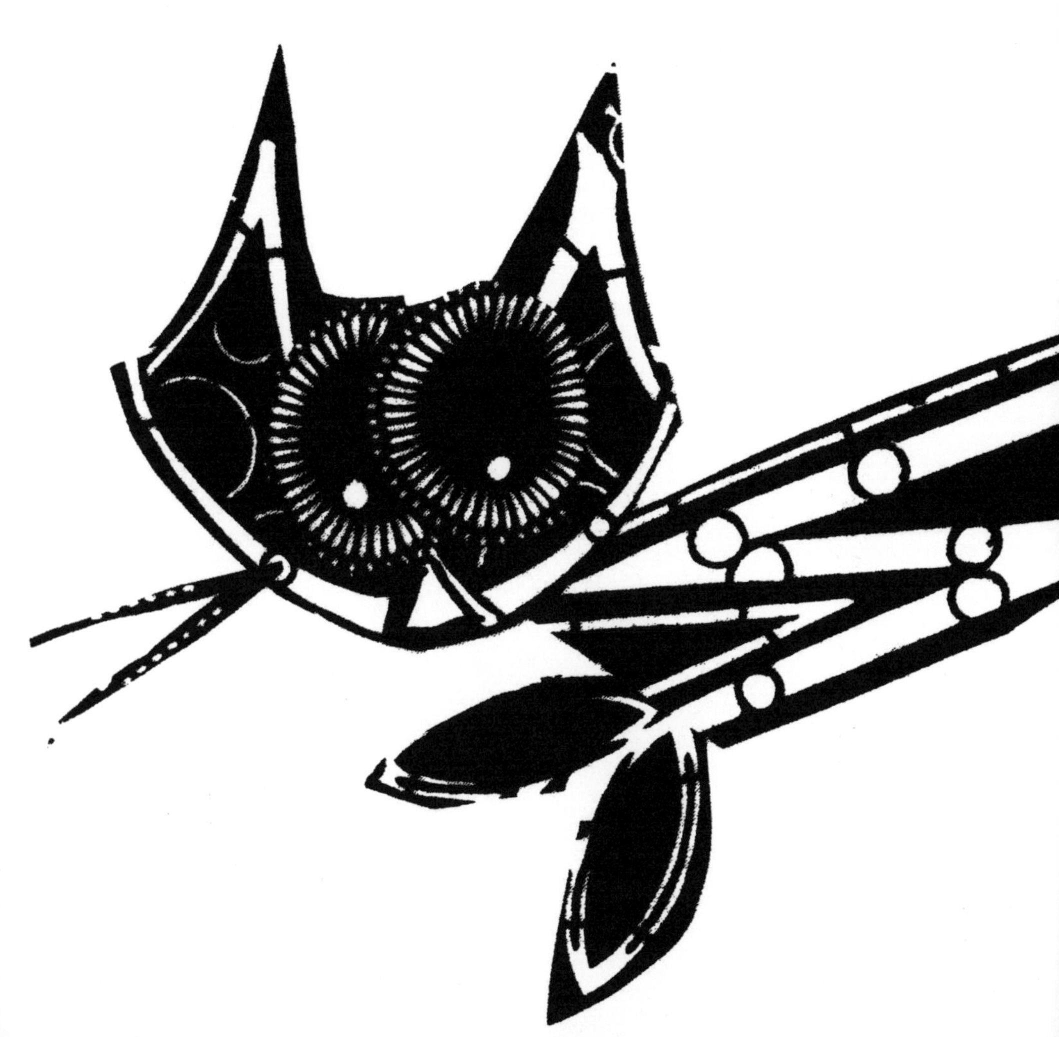

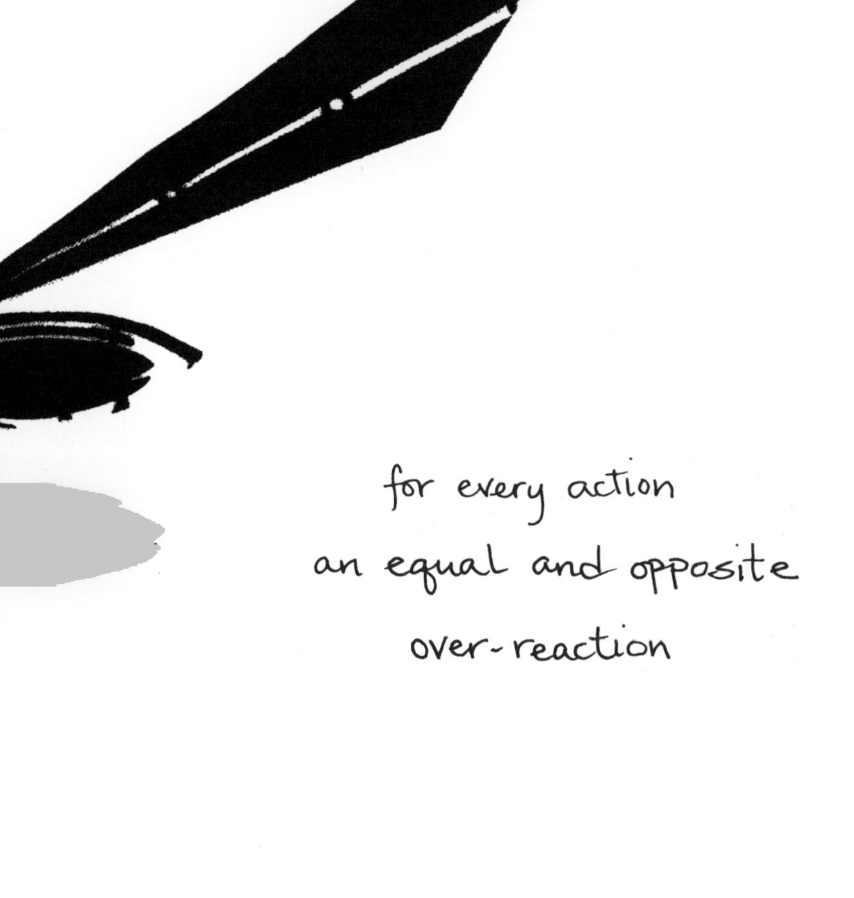
for every action
an equal and opposite
over-reaction

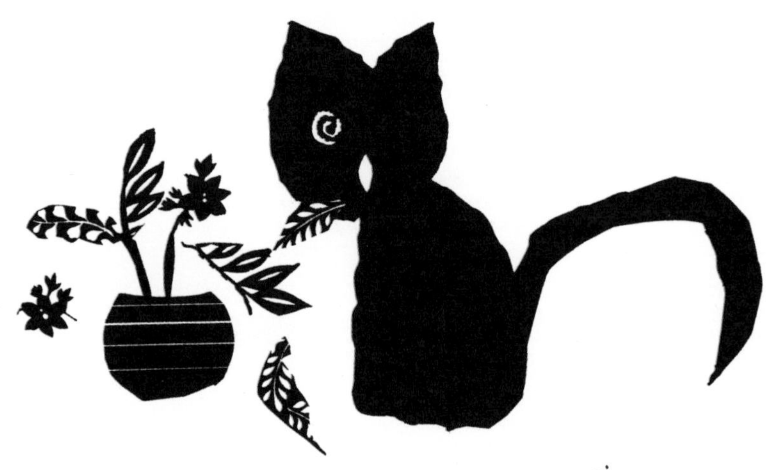

though you're the diva
chewing the scenery is
considered bad form

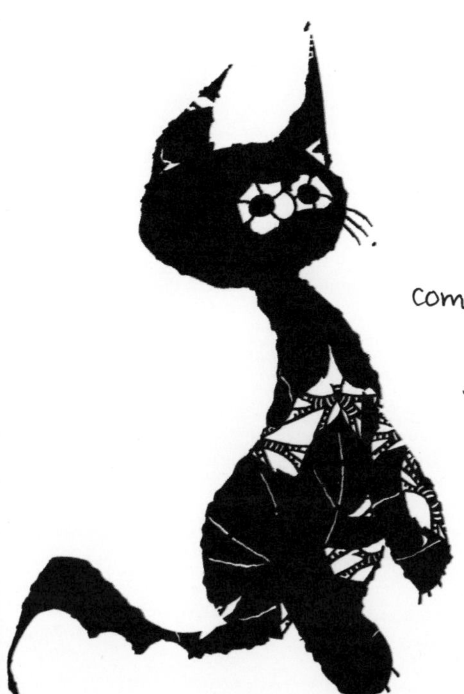

highly eccentric
compellingly weird – one cat
just workin' the room

it's someone special
who can turn a bad hair day
into a statement

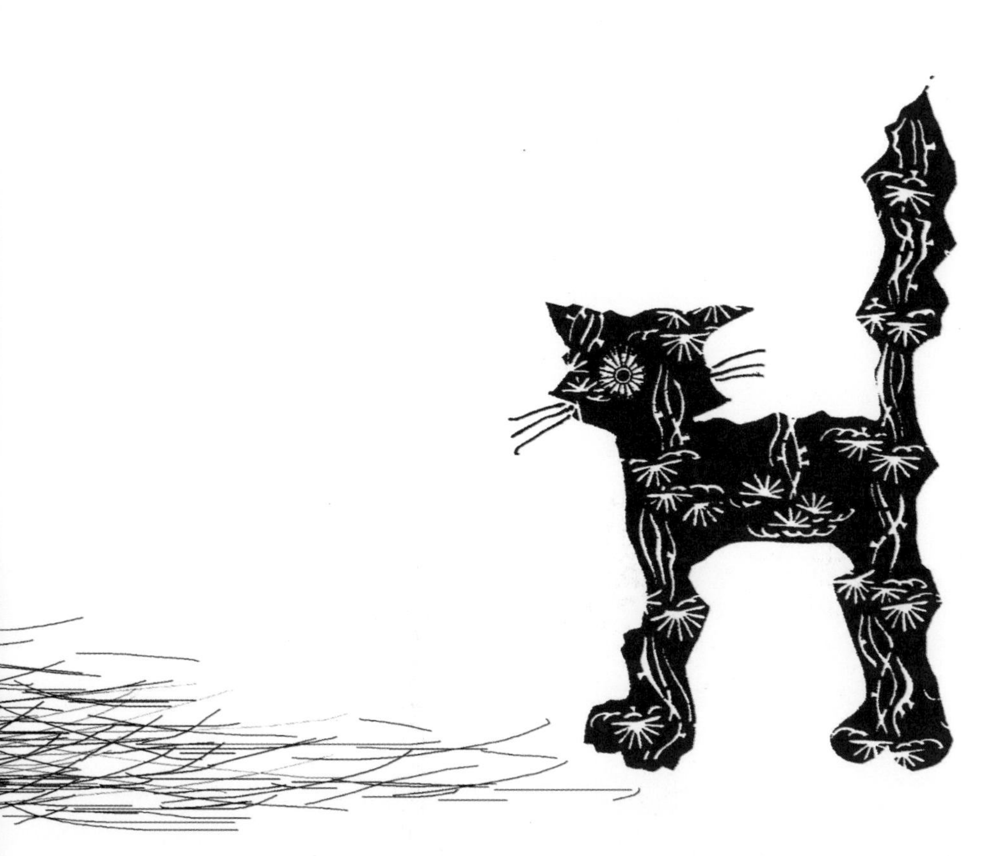

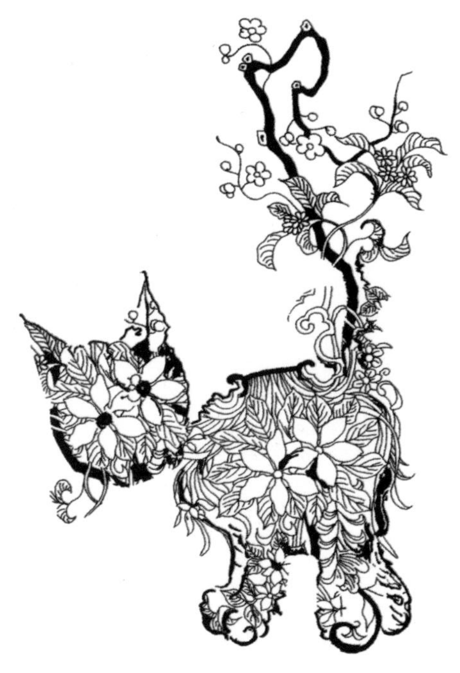

tend to your garden

dig in the dirt — by all means

get lost in the weeds

funny curious
authentic independent
she's your role model

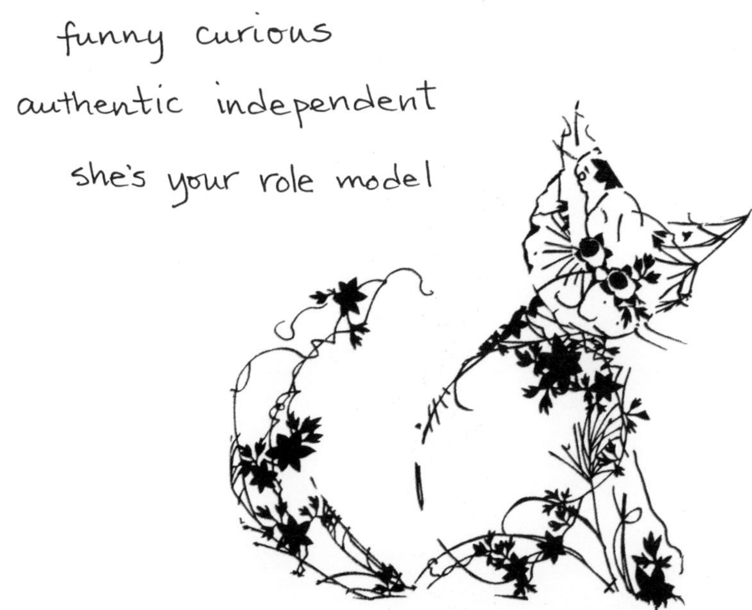

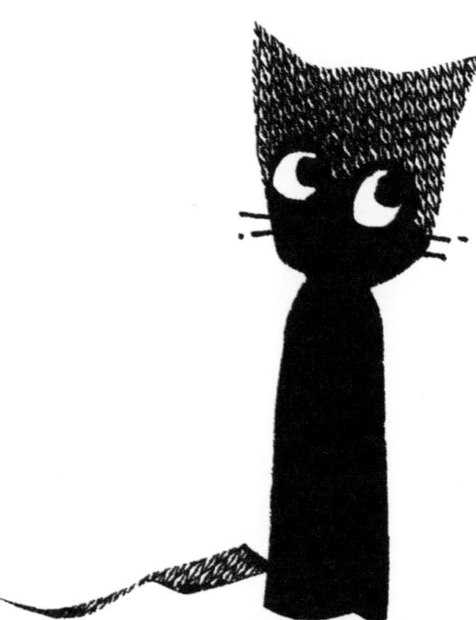
every meal you make
every holiday you take —
someone's watching you

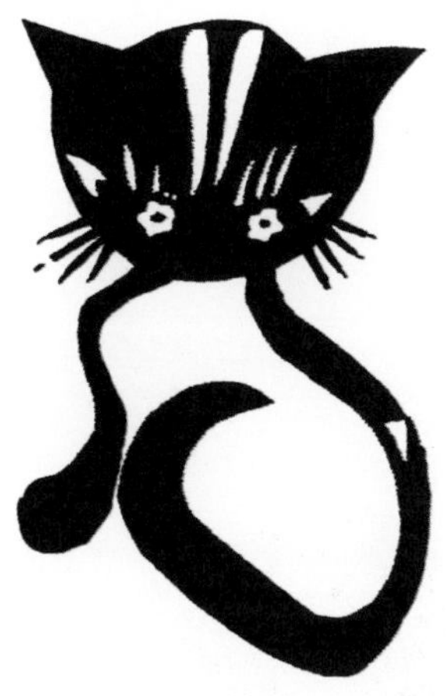

you fed me dinner
but don't get too familiar
"NO" really means "NO"

empty cardboard box

endless possibilities

life is so simple

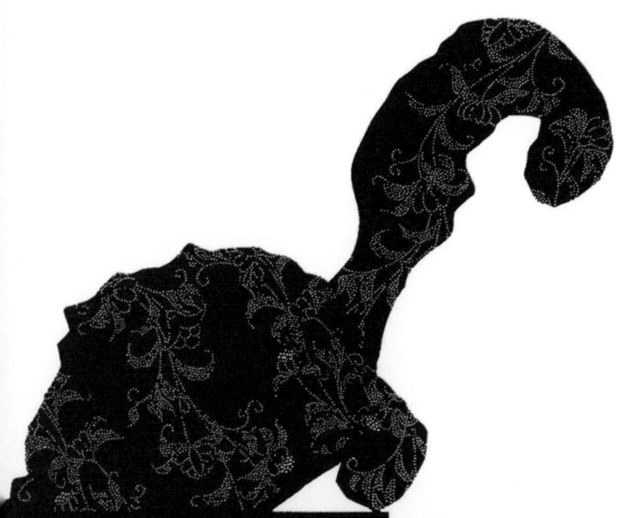

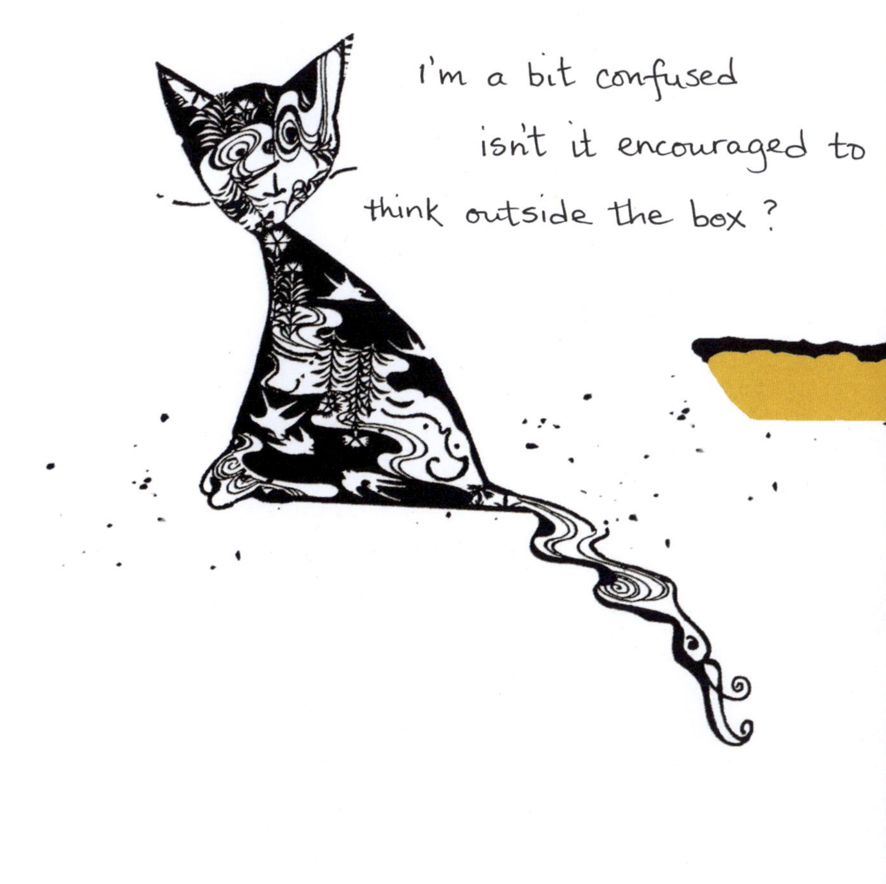

I'm a bit confused
isn't it encouraged to
think outside the box ?

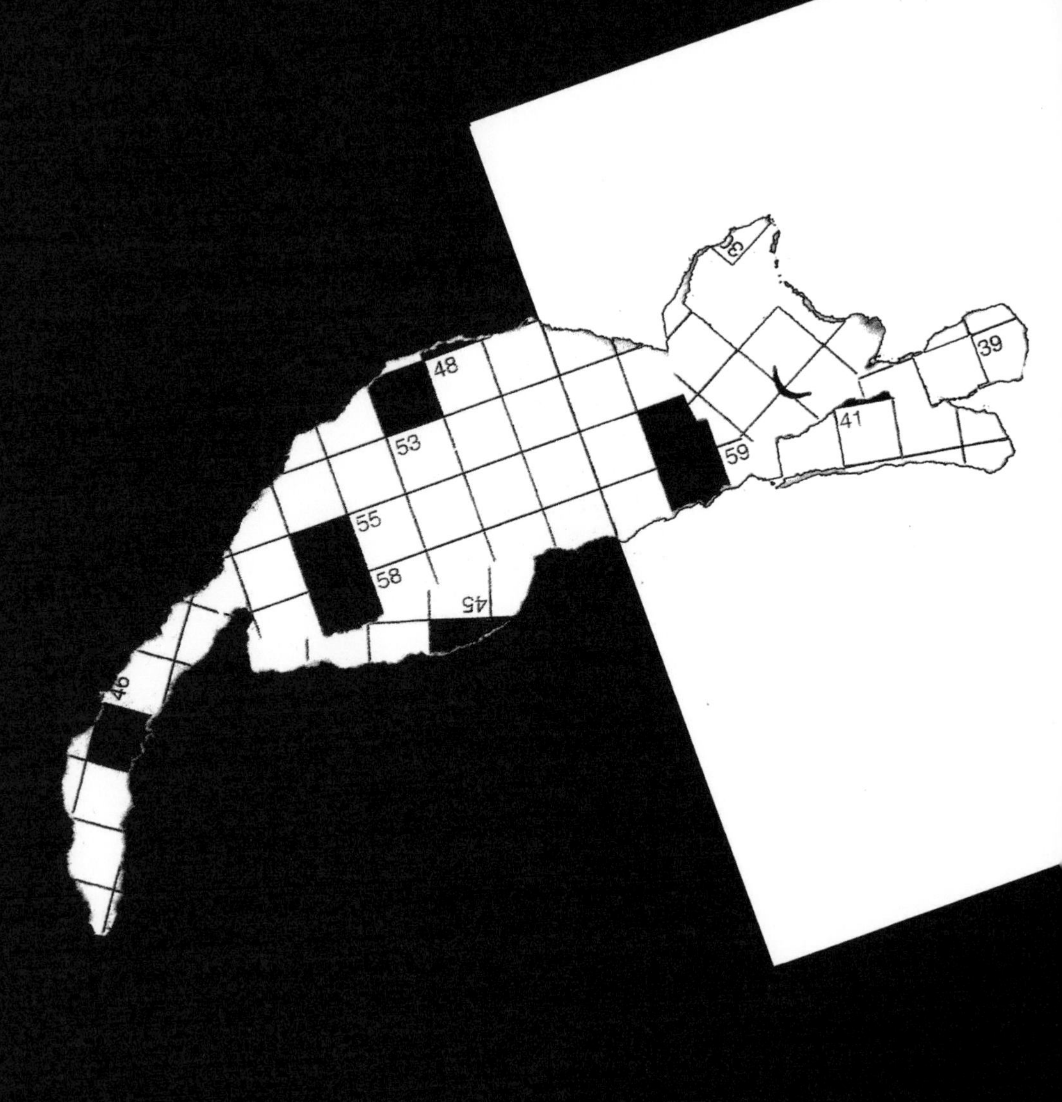

SHARE THE CEREAL
PERUSE THE MORNING PAPER
CO-OPT THE
CROSSWORD

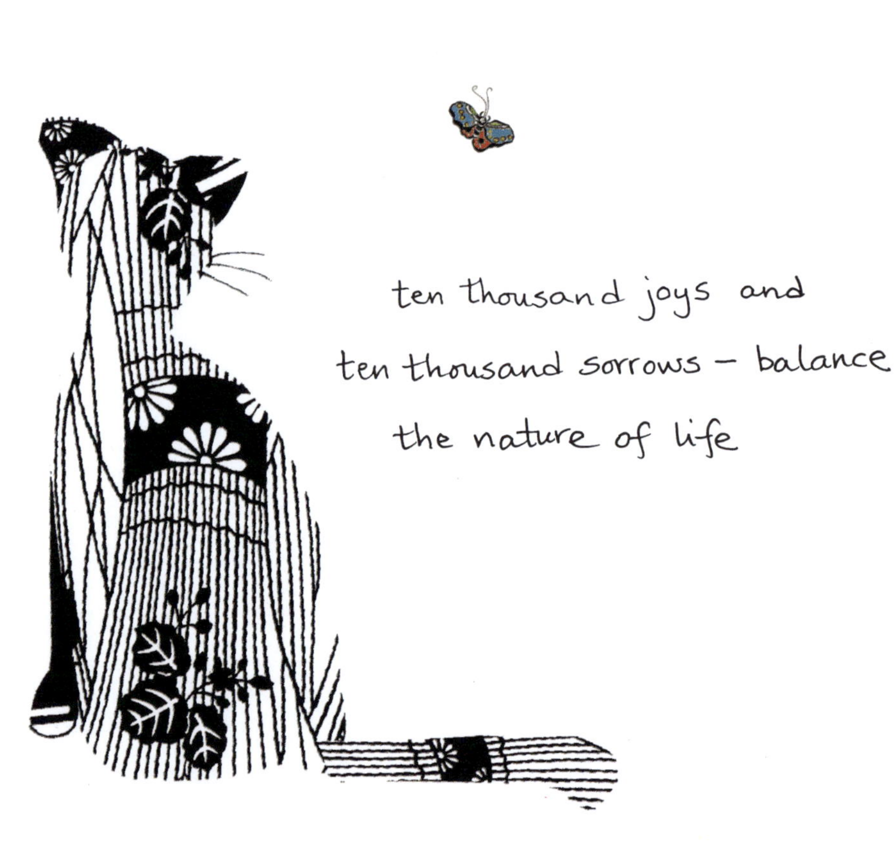

ten thousand joys and
ten thousand sorrows – balance
the nature of life

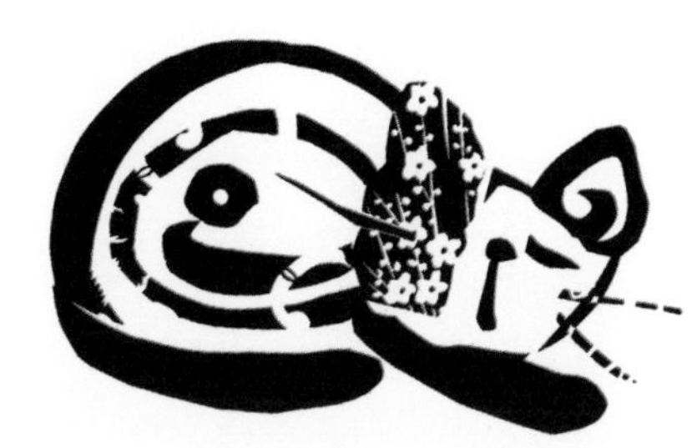

solitary night

alone with the cat — warm bed

good book — nirvana

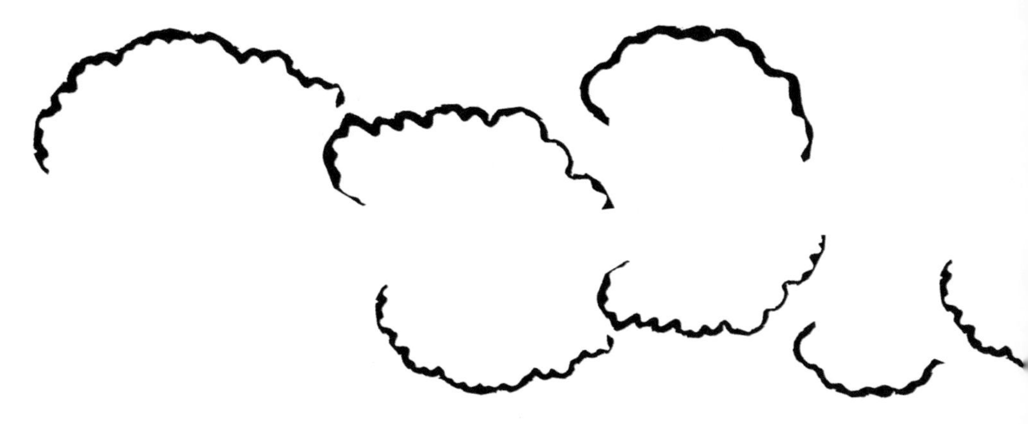

weather changes — no
matter what the forecast it
will be reigning cats

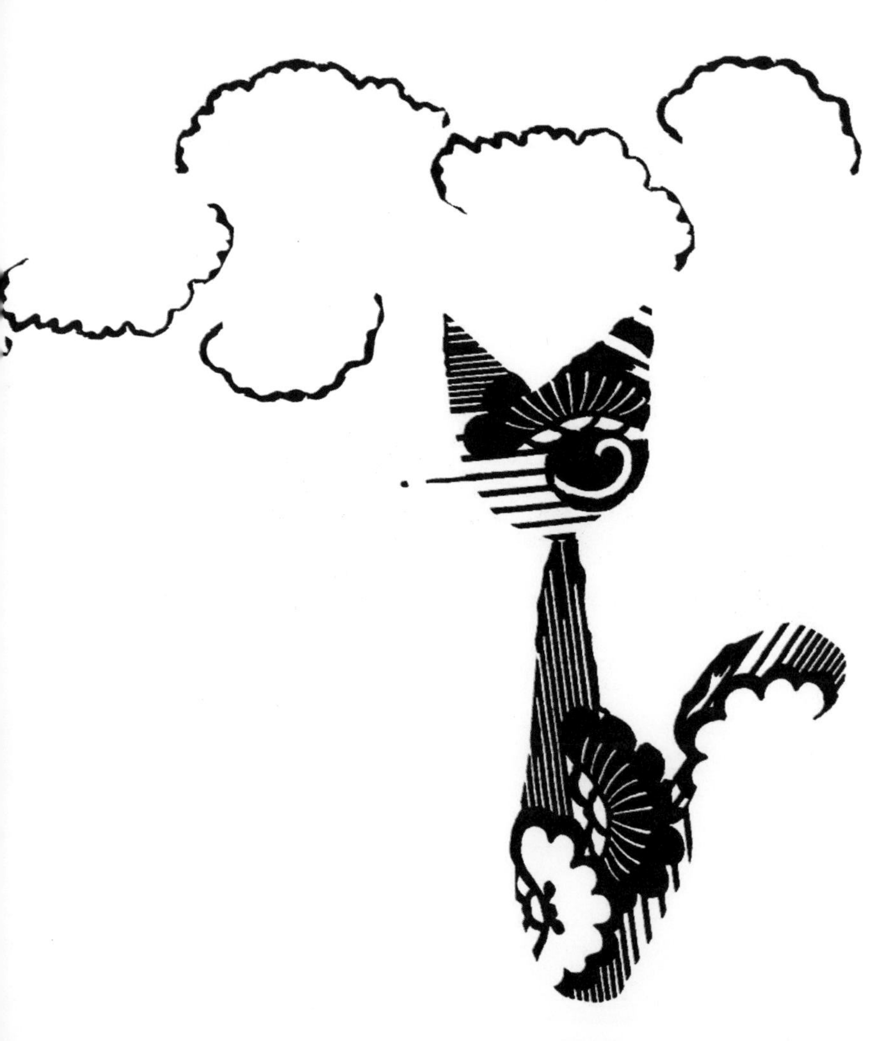

almost anything
can be made better by the
laying on of paws

wabi sabi – those
cracks in us that let the light
shine in and shine out

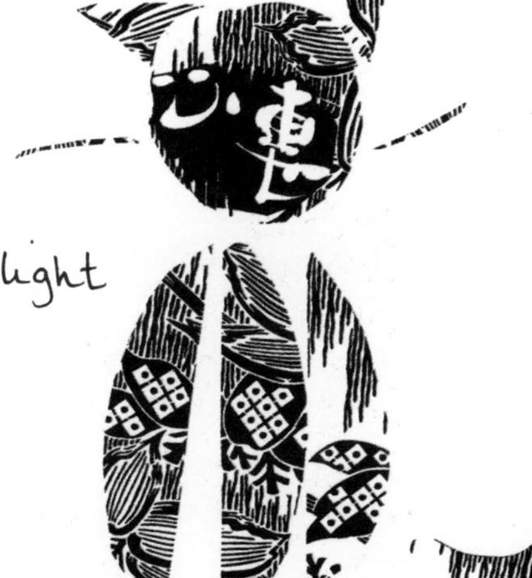

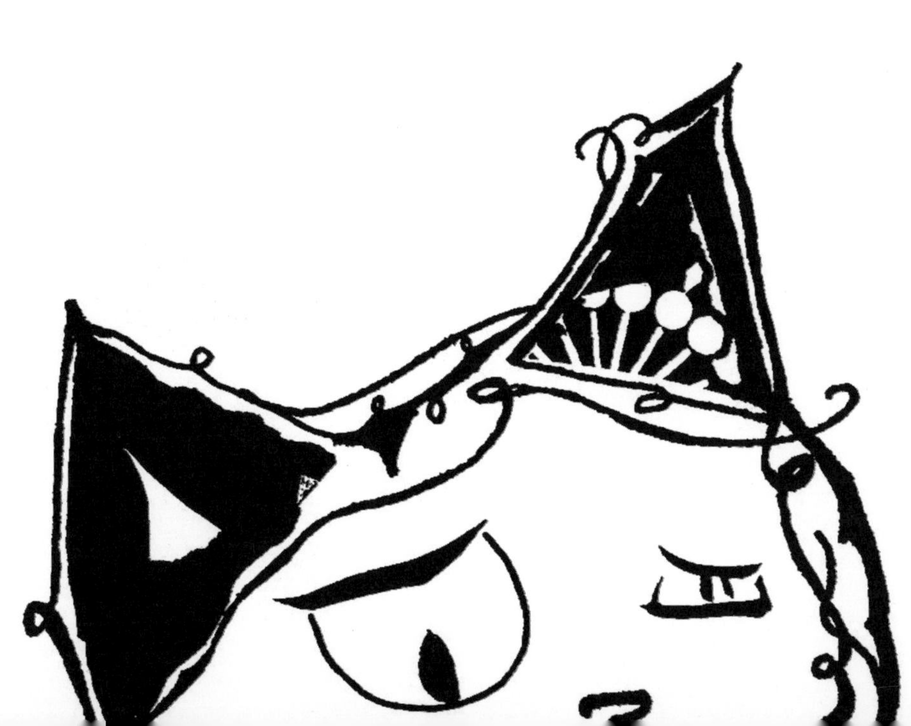

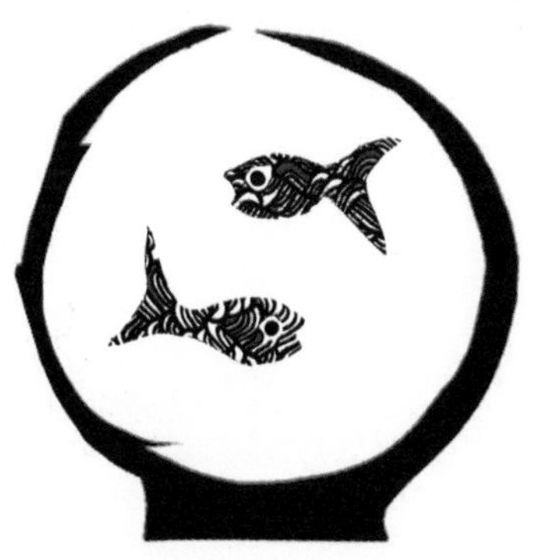

curiosity
the key ingredient to
any life well lived

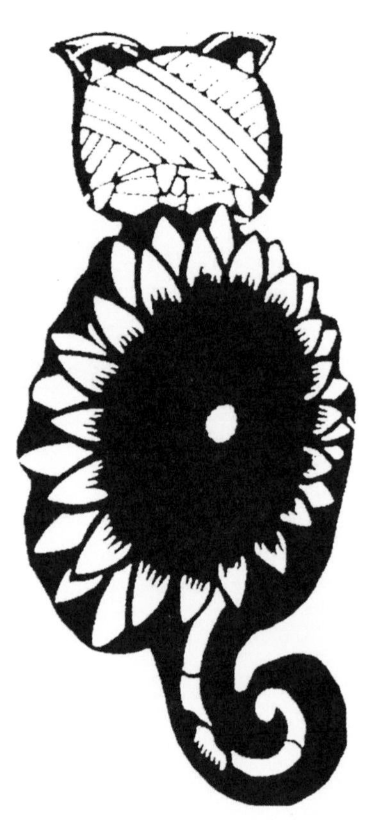

you have forgotten

my abandonment issues

I've forgotten you

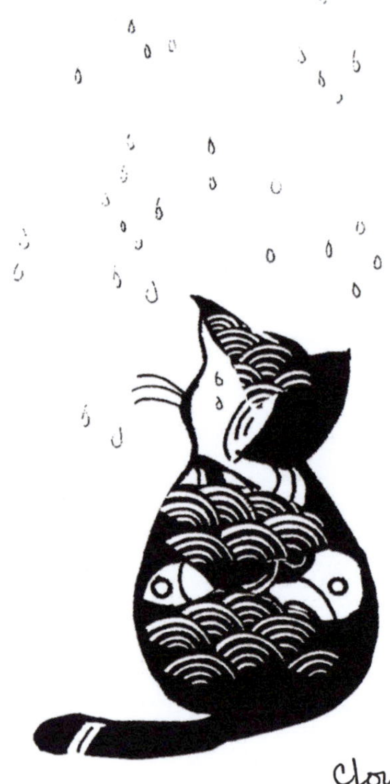

cloudy skies above
down pour soon to follow

no rain

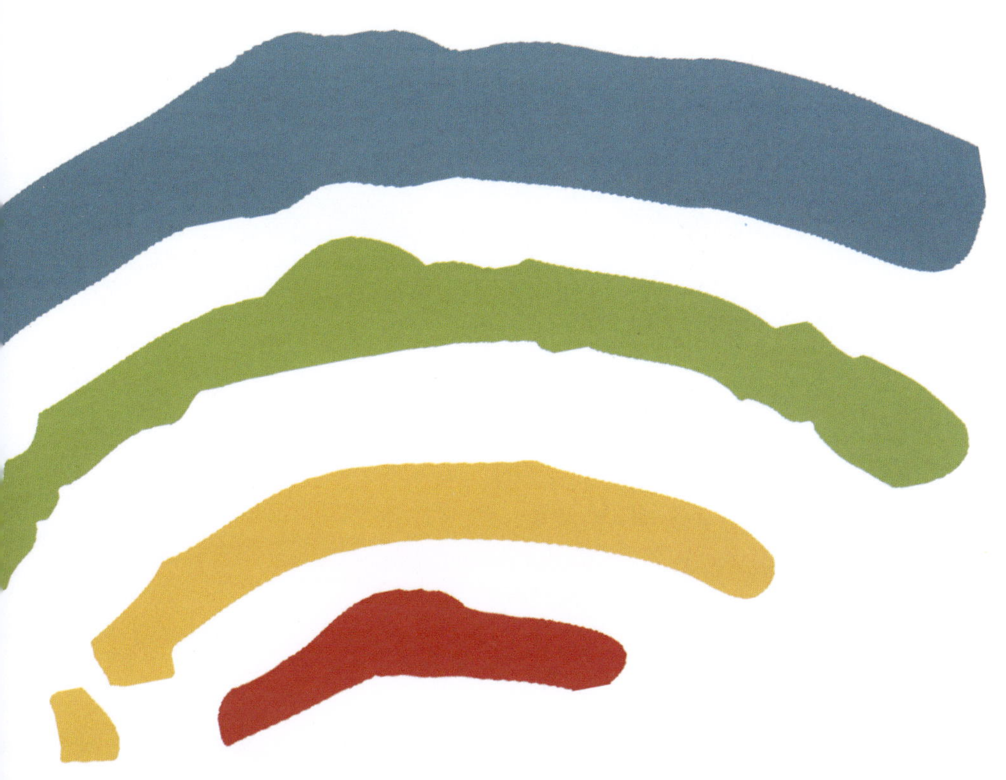

no rainbows

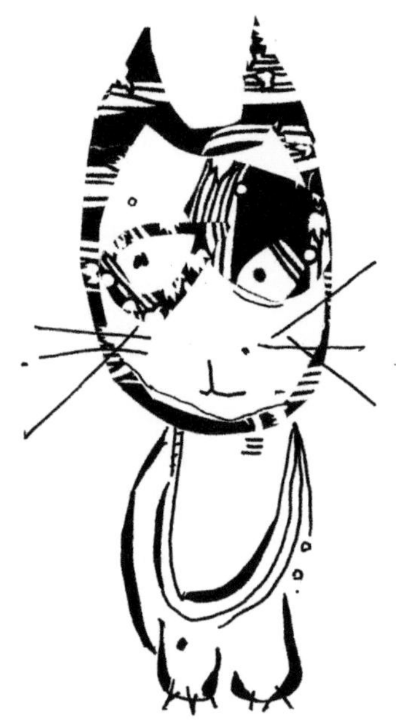

a self-respecting

kitty cat will never cast

her purrs before swine

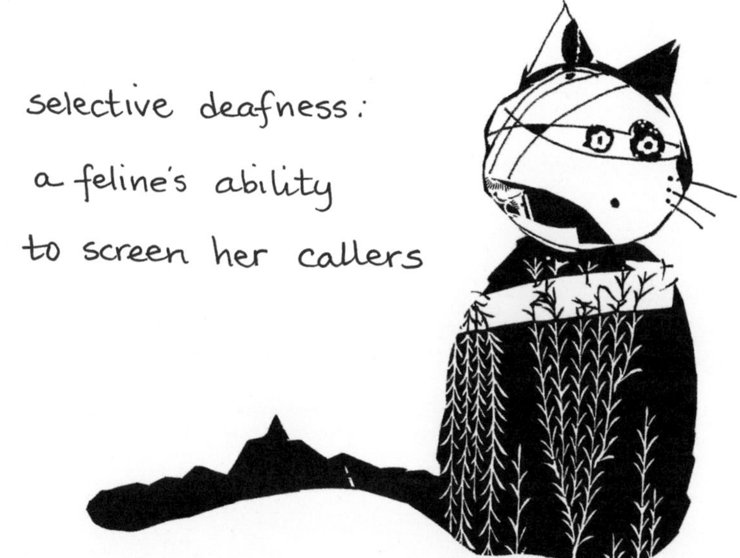

selective deafness:

a feline's ability

to screen her callers

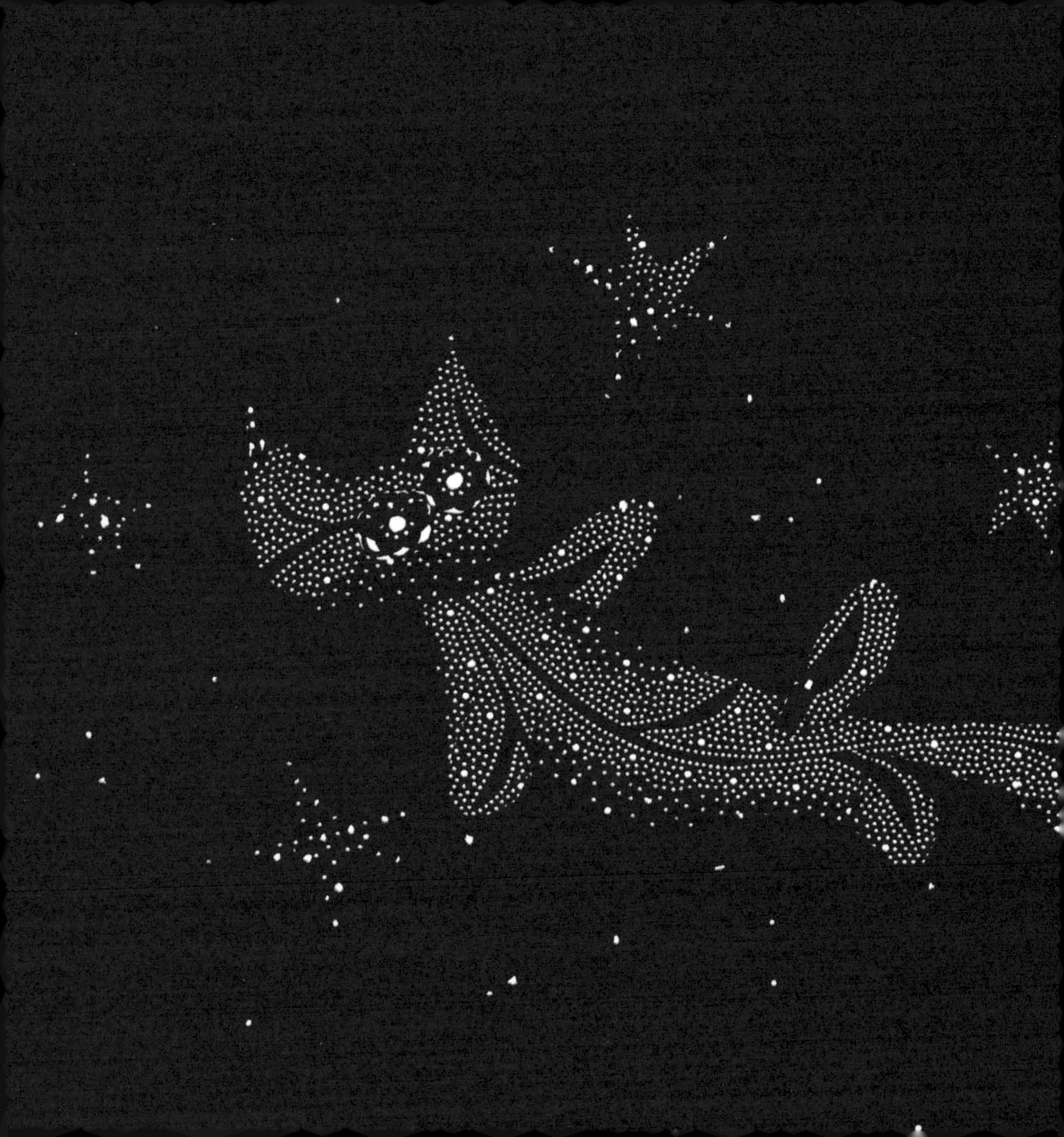

look up – dream your dreams

make all your wishes – the stars

are always shining

wee small morning hours
the house is much too quiet
let the games begin

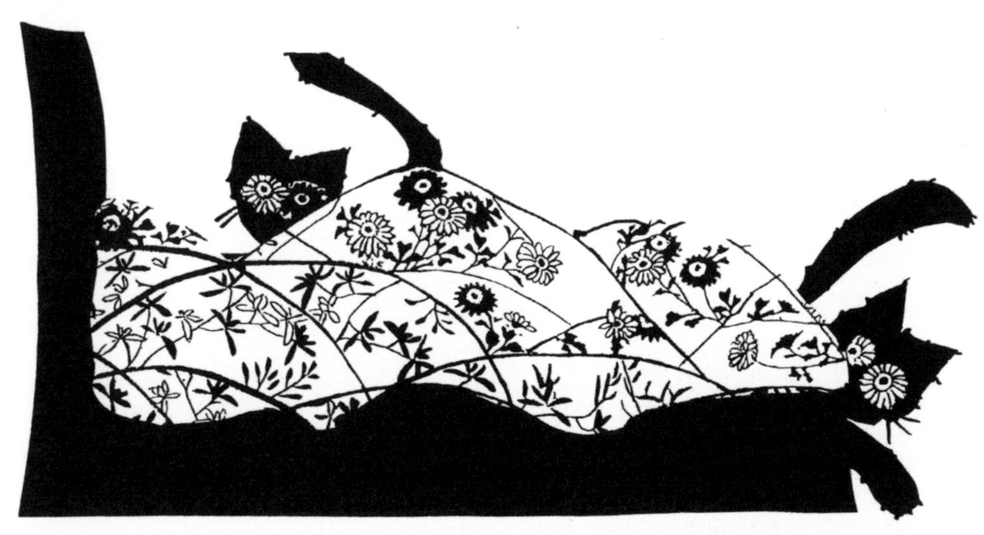

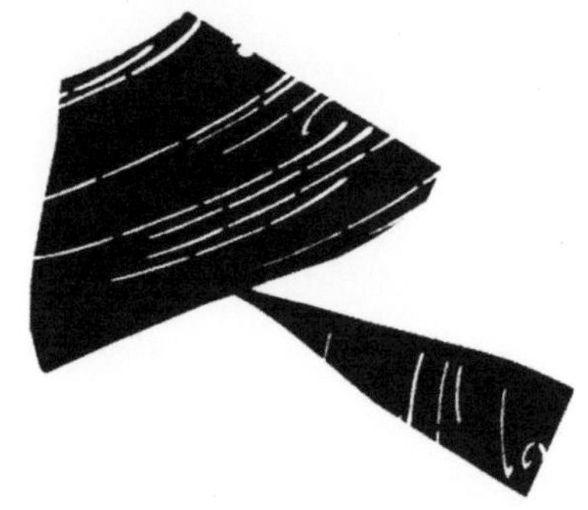
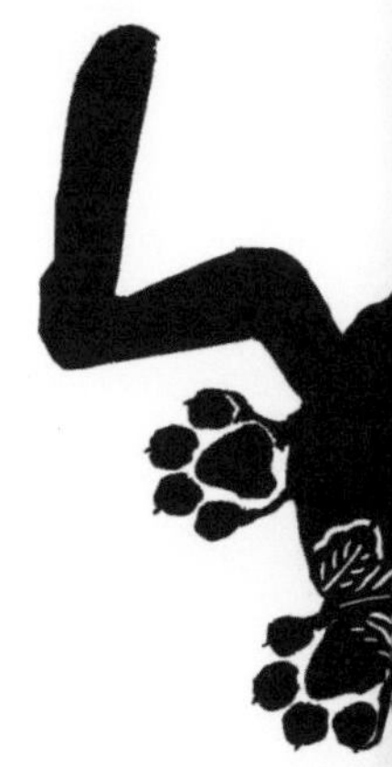

remove obstacles

transform energy — feng shui

household harmony

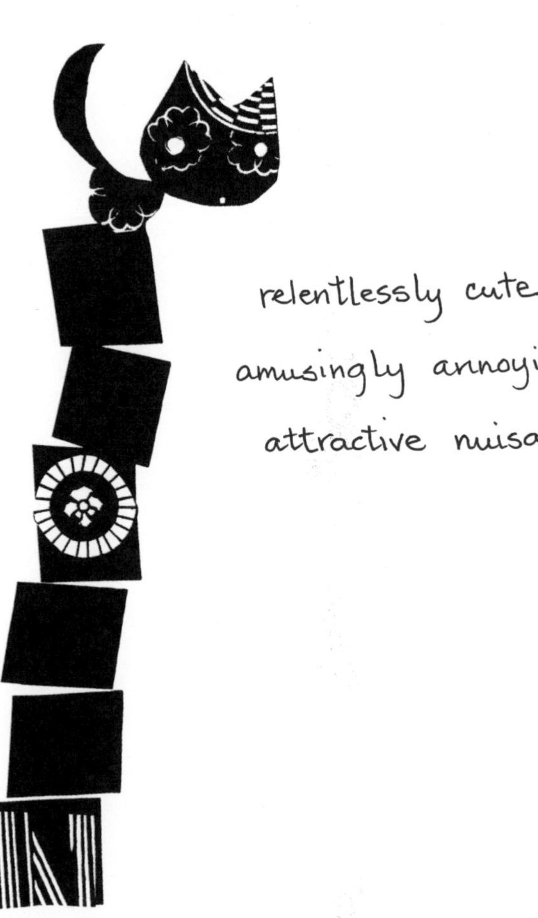

relentlessly cute

amusingly annoying

attractive nuisance

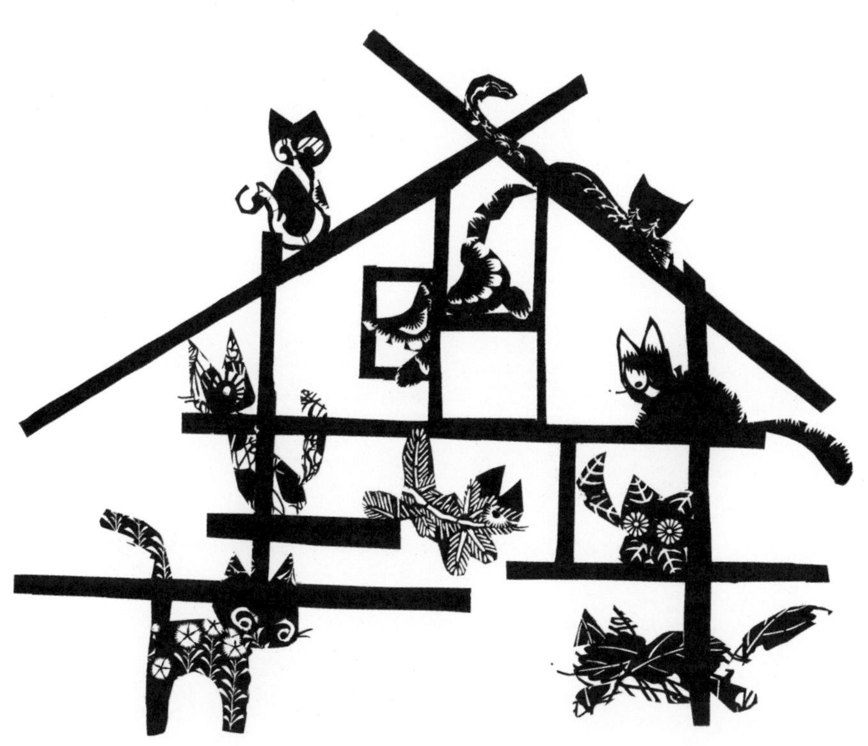

one cat's a comfort

two cat's sublime — four or more

a clear lifestyle choice

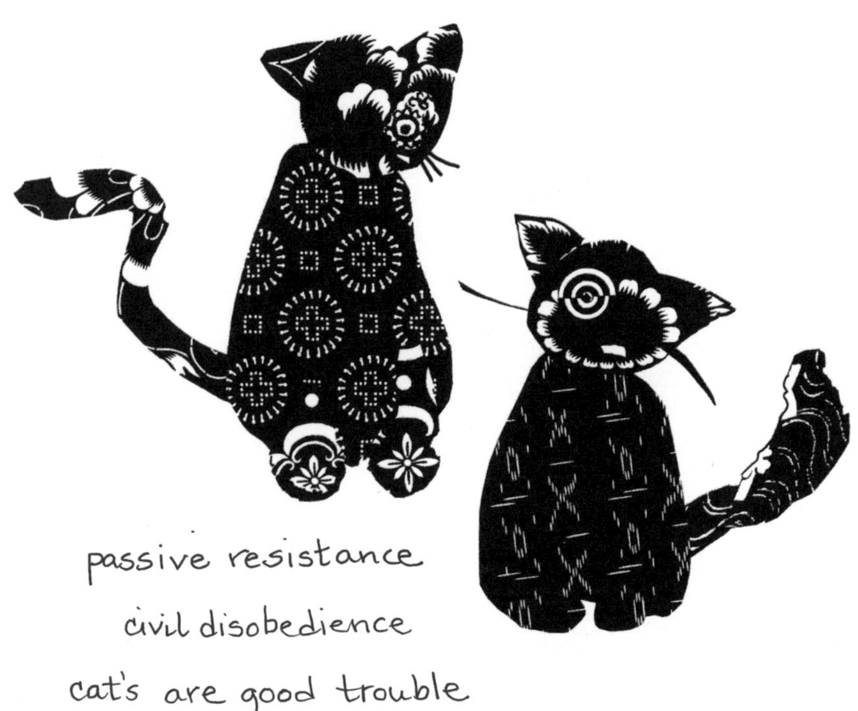

passive resistance
civil disobedience
cat's are good trouble

the magnetism

of neatly folded laundry

cannot be denied

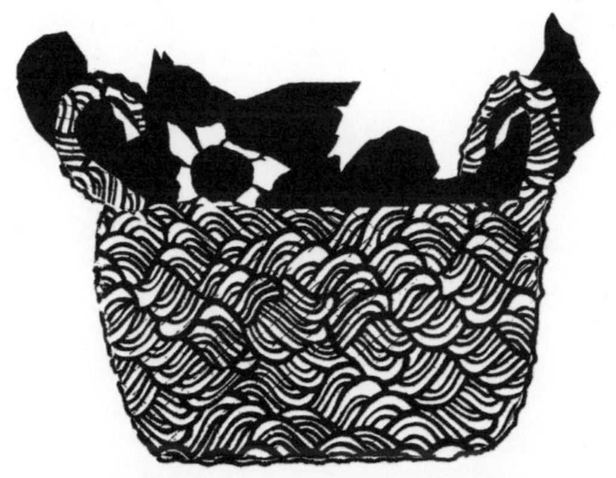

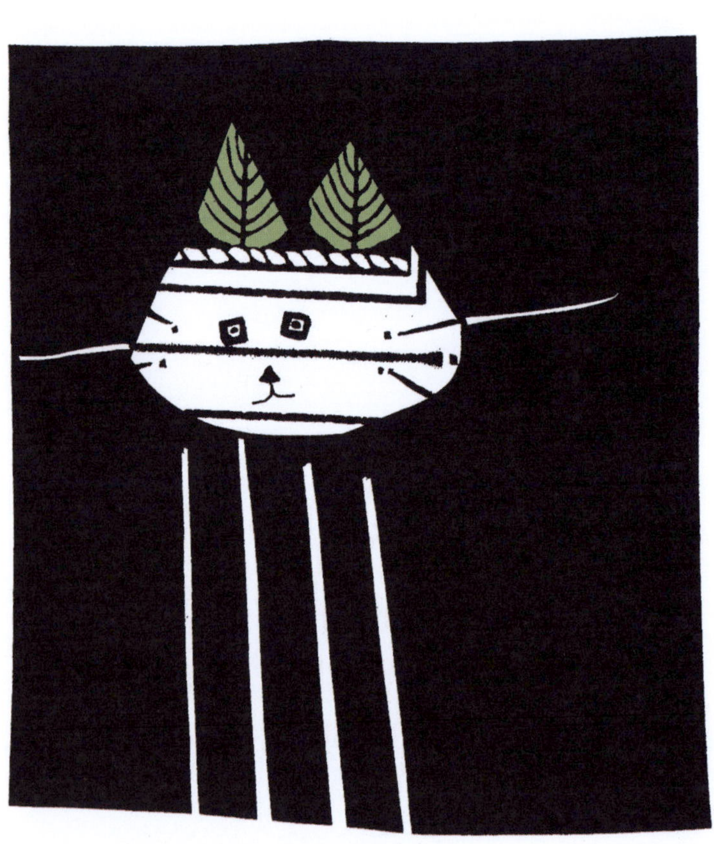

New Resolutions:

Play more. Accommodate less.

Commit to naptime.

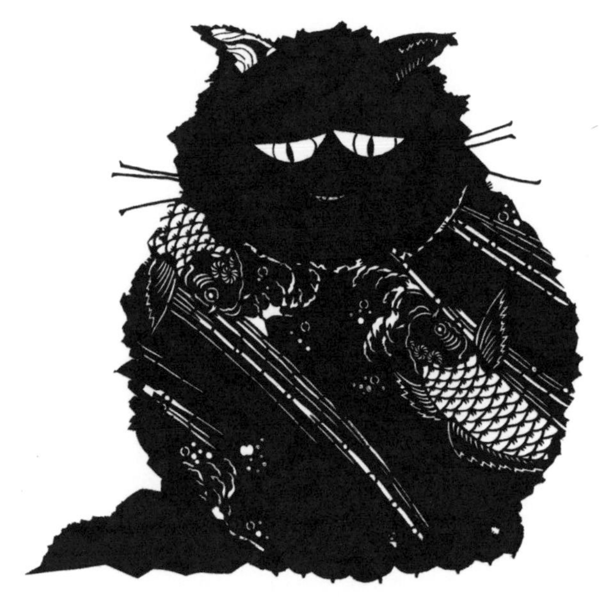

daily conundrum:

live life to the fullest or

stay on the diet

every now and then

the situation calls for

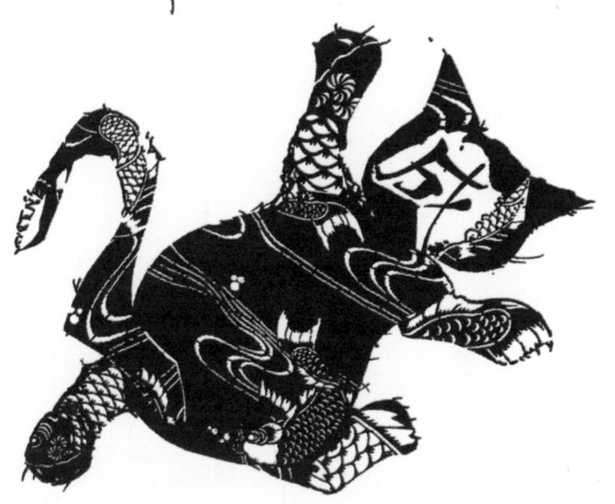

reckless abandon

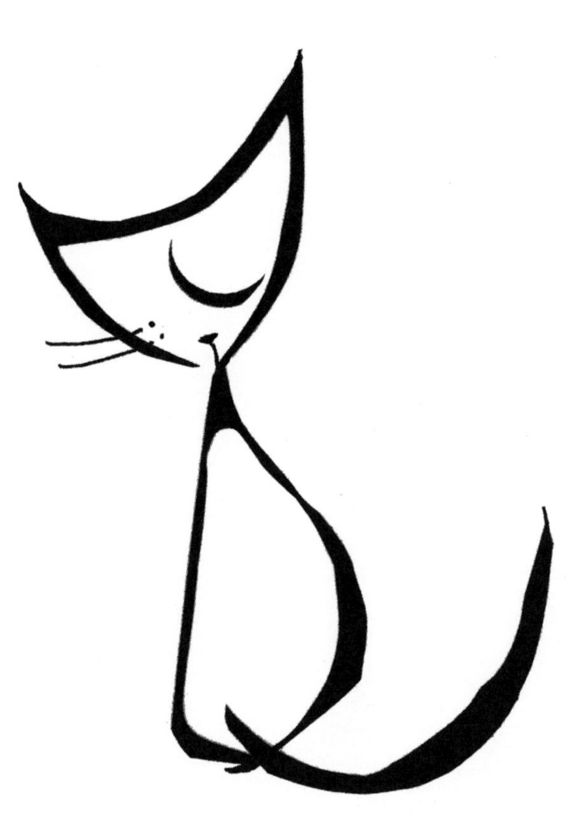

less is often more
simplify your life and you
will be happier

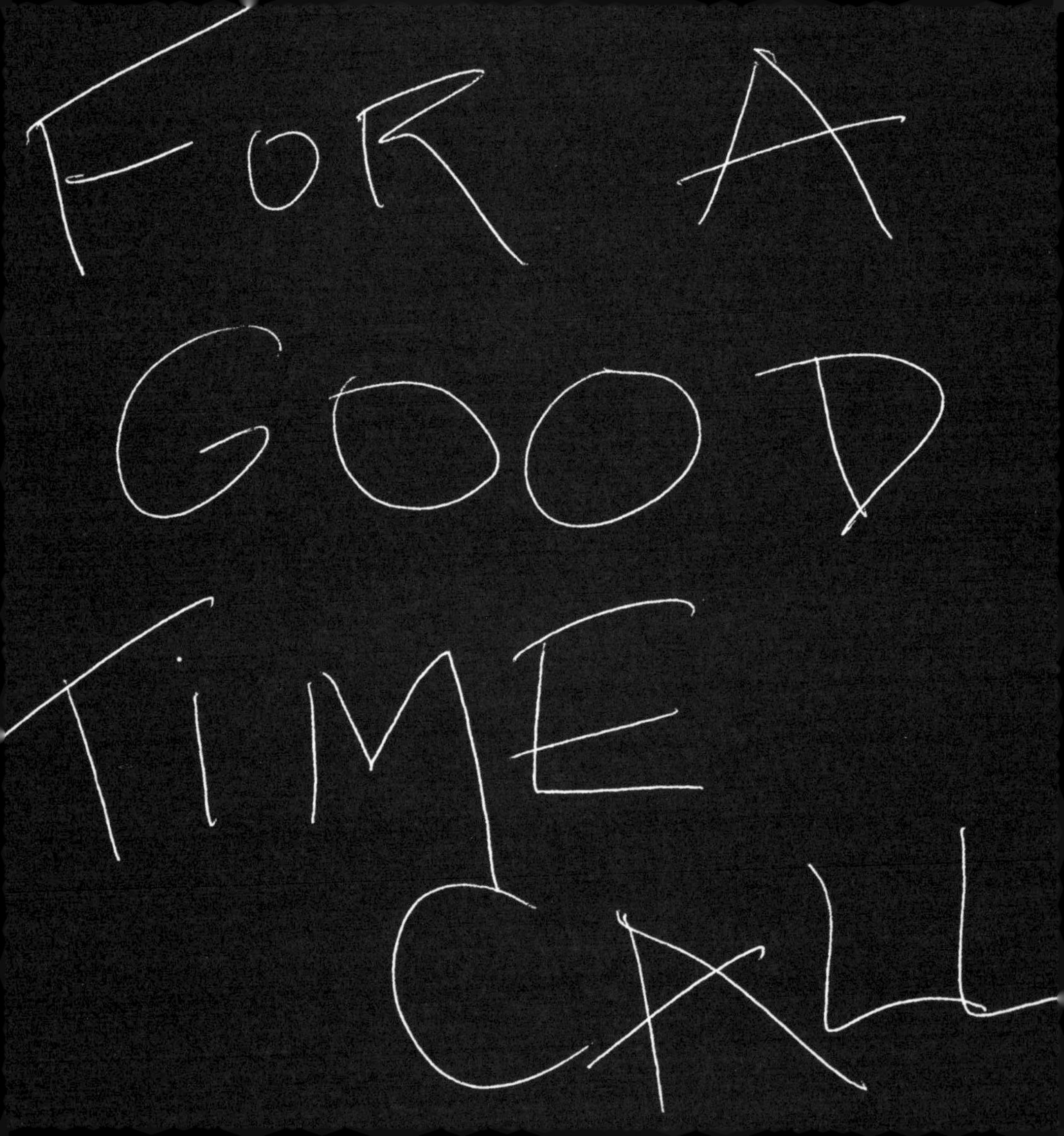

FOR A
GOOD
TIME
CALL

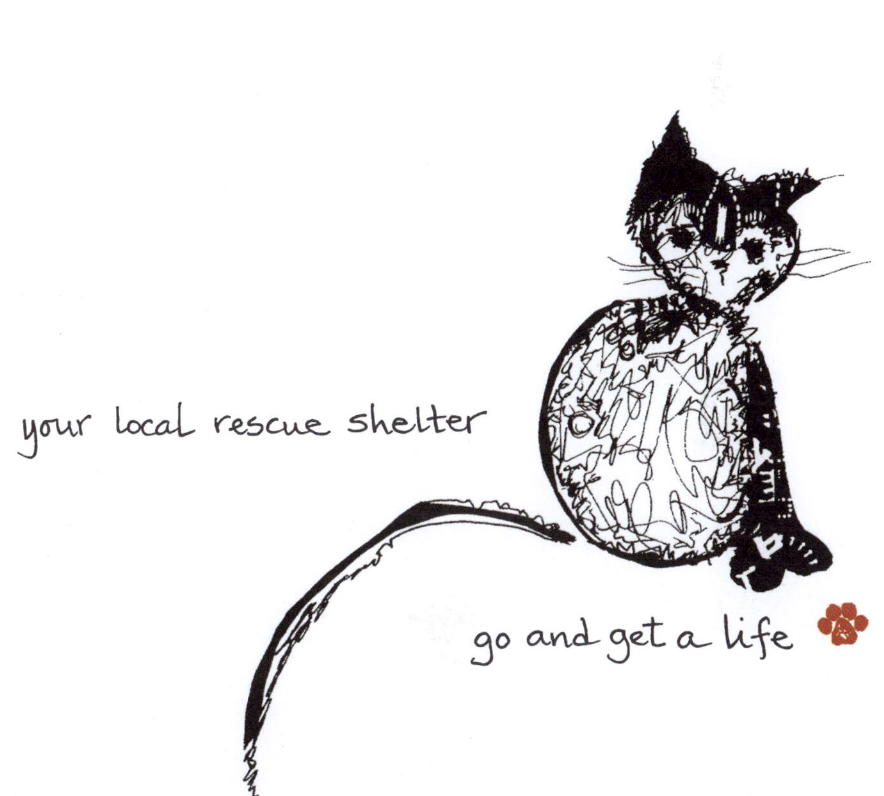
your local rescue shelter
go and get a life

Published by Tuttle Publishing, an imprint of Periplus Editions (HK) Ltd.

www.tuttlepublishing.com

978-4-8053-2059-4

Distributed by:

North America, Latin America & Europe
Tuttle Publishing
364 Innovation Drive
North Clarendon; VT 05759-9436 U.S.A.
Tel: (802) 773-8930; Fax: (802) 773-6993
info@tuttlepublishing.com
www.tuttlepublishing.com

Japan
Tuttle Publishing
Yaekari Building 3rd Floor
5-4-12 Osaki Shinagawa-ku
Tokyo 141 0032
Tel: (81) 3 5437-0171
Fax: (81) 3 5437-0755
sales@tuttle.co.jp; www.tuttle.co.jp

Asia Pacific
Berkeley Books Pte. Ltd.
3 Kallang Sector, #04-01
Singapore 349278
Tel: (65) 6741-2178
Fax: (65) 6741-2179
inquiries@periplus.com.sg
www.tuttlepublishing.com

Printed in China   2604CM
29 28 27 26   5 4 3 2 1

GPSR Representative
Matt Parsons, matt.parsons@upi2mbooks.hr, UPI-2M PLUS d.o.o., Medulićeva 20, 10000 Zagreb, Croatia

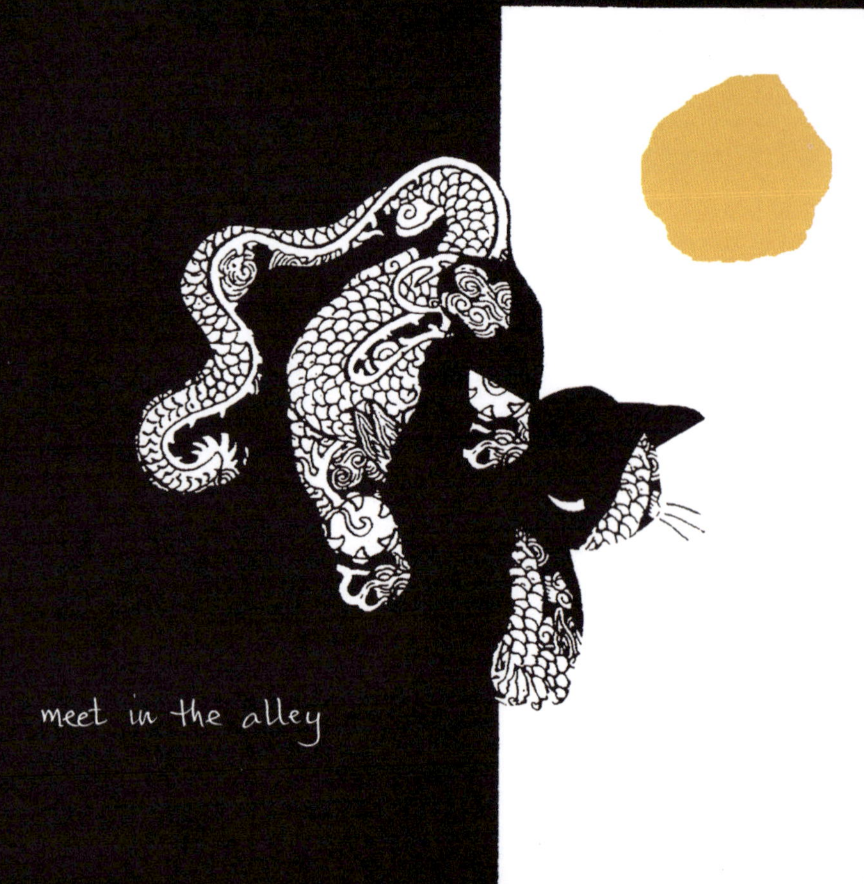

meet in the alley